D0428058

PRAISE FOR **Welcome to the Family!**

The pages of this work reflect the author who lives up to the title of her splendid book, *Welcome to the Family!* It is a warm, informal and lucid introduction to Jewish living and embraces the reader with useful information in a personal mode. It has something important to say to spiritual seekers of Judaism whether they are unsynagogued or unchurched, Jewishly married or intermarried.
Rabbi Harold Schulweis, spiritual leader, Valley Beth Shalom, Encino, California.

Mitzvah. I learned from *Welcome to the Family!* that mitzvah means, among other things "a good deed." Lois Shenker has done all non-Jewish families whose sons or daughters are marrying Jews a good deed, and then some, by writing this book. My wife and I had so many questions when my son (a Christian) announced he was going to marry a Jewish woman. "What will the wedding be like?" "What do Jews believe?" "What are the different approaches to Judaism?" "What practices and holidays might our grandchildren observe?"

Welcome to the Family! answered these questions for us in a clear and straightforward manner. I was particularly pleased with its positive message, as many books we had read about intermarriage focused on the negatives, neglecting to inform the reader about the basic facts of the Jewish experience. I wanted to learn more about Jews and the Jewish experience, and this book encouraged my interest. After reading it, I did feel welcomed into the family.

I highly recommend this book to anyone who wishes to learn more about the Jewish experience—those contemplating intermarriage, their parents, relatives and friends, and anyone else who want to understand their Jewish friends and colleagues better.
JEFFREY G. MILLER, Associate Dean, Boston University School of Management

Welcome to the Family!

Welcome to the Family!
Opening Doors to the Jewish Experience

Lois Sussman Shenker

White Cloud Press
Ashland, Oregon

Printed in the United States of America

First edition: 2001

01 02 03 04   1 2 3 4 5 6

Cover design: Blackfish Creative
Cover photo: Greg Kozawa

Photo credits: Images by Floom (pp. 39, 40, 42, 87, 98, 111, 113, 114,
115-top, 117); Jewish Federation of Portland (pp. 31); Portland Jewish
Academy (p. 81-bottom, 85); Portland Jewish Review (p. 35, 45, 81-top,
84, 87, 90, 92, 96); courtesy of Lee and Sheri Cordova (p. 60); courtesy
of Rabbi Daniel and Carol Isaak (p. 53); photo by Brian Kramer
Photography courtesy of Mark Rubin and Leah Rubin (p. 61); courtesy
of White Cloud Press, reprinted from *God's Middlemen: A Habad
Retrospective* by Reuven Alpert (p. 29); courtesy of the author (p. 115).

LIBRARY OF CONGRESS CATALOGING IN PUBLICATION DATA
Shenker, Lois Sussman
    Welcome to the Family: opening doors to the Jewish experience /
Lois Sussman Shenker.
        p. cm.
    ISBN: 1-883991-41-2
    1. Judaism. I. Title.

    BM561 .S48 2001
    296--dc21

                                        2001045550

Dedication

To Debbie, Tracey, and Bill,
whom we were blessed to welcome into our family

TABLE OF CONTENTS

ACKNOWLEDGMENTS

My deep thanks and appreciation to:

• The rabbis of the Introduction to Judaism Class: My own Jewish beliefs and practices have been validated, clarified, added to, and enriched by your knowledge.

• The many students of the Introduction to Judaism class who continue to inspire me.

• All of my many readers, whose input was so helpful. Special thanks to Rabbi Daniel Isaak, Irene Hecht, Tom Fields-Meyer, and Diana Ayton-Shenker.

• The professionals: Sharon Castlen, the first professional to read my manuscript and encourage me ever since, Diane Solomon, Dorothy Wall, and Sherri Emmons for their editing skills, Elana Brazile for her computer expertise, Blackfish Creative Design for their great cover design, and Steven Scholl, my publisher, who was willing to take a chance on an unknown author because he believed in my book.

• The Kessler family for so graciously opening the door of my childhood home for the cover photo.

• My dear parents, who gave me Jewish roots and nurtured them with love.

• All those who have shared my Jewish experience, making it all the more meaningful to me.

• Our precious children: Joel and Debbie, Diana and Bill, Jordan and Tracey, and grandchildren: Mandy, Joshua, Matthew, Rachel, Sarah, Benjamin, Lizzie, and Eli. You are our greatest joy.

• First, last, and always, my husband Arden, my partner in the creation of our Jewish home and family, my personal font of knowledge, sounding board, reader, editor, critic, support, best friend, and sweetest love.

Introduction
In the Beginning

"*If something terrible happens, God forbid,*" our non-Jewish daughter-in-law anguished to our son, "*What will I do? I've never been to a Jewish funeral!*" Our son was about to travel across the country for his father's bypass surgery.

It was Debbie's discomfort in not knowing what to expect or what was expected of her that convinced me to write this book. I wrote it for her, for her family and friends, for my children's non-Jewish in-laws, and for all those with Jewish connections who want to understand and know more about the Jewish experience. My goal is to provide basic information about Judaism and things Jewish in an easy-to-understand format, and so help non-Jews and others who want to know feel more comfortable when attending Jewish events and interacting with Jewish people.

Welcome to the Family!

As both the facilitator and administrator for the Oregon Board of Rabbis' Introduction to Judaism Course, I have worked with more than 800 adult students since I began writing this book. They come to the course seeking information about Judaism, for many reasons. Some are becoming Jewish, some are entering into an intermarriage or are already in one, some are beginning to reclaim their Jewish heritage after reaching adulthood. Regardless of why they come, they all are seeking to increase their comfort level with the Jewish experience. As I have worked with them, it has become clear that their families and friends are seeking to be comfortable, too.

I chose Welcome *to the Family!* as the title for my book because it was written as a personal welcome to *you* as you seek information about the Jewish experience, for whatever reason. I also chose it because I have extended this welcome in my own life, in my own family.

Through the marriages of our children, my husband and I have welcomed three *new* children into our family, none of whom was born to Judaism. Since Debbie, Tracey, and Bill have been with us, I have been both partner in and observer of the changes in their lives as they have blended their backgrounds with ours. Over the years there have been countless discussions about what it means to be Jewish—with them, with members of their families, and with our grown up granddaughter Mandy, as she has come to terms with her Catholic upbringing and our family's beliefs. We have discussed everything from, "So why don't you guys believe in Jesus?" (from 11-year-old Mandy) to "What do you believe about life after death?"

I have watched and participated as Tracey adjusted to

her life as a Jew by choice and as Debbie and Bill have learned about and joined our family's Jewish observances and customs. I am grateful that they have felt comfortable asking questions, and even more grateful that they are providing those answers for their children. I *kvell* (Yiddish for take great pleasure) over the Jewishness they now create in their own homes. Most of all, I appreciate the respect they and their families have always given to our Jewish heritage.

These new families are forging a new kind of experience, unlike the ones in which either parent was raised. I believe in their future, and in those of so many young families like them. I hope their futures will be enhanced by this book, and that I will be privileged to continue as a part of their families' memories and Jewish experience.

As I look back on my earliest memories, many of them I shared with my *Bubbe* (Yiddish for grandmother). I remember stories she told me about the old country and her family when my father was a boy. I remember Yiddish words she used. She almost always called me *Shayna Punim* (pretty face) instead of Lois. (When she did use my name, her immigrant accented speech turned Lois into Louisl.) I remember the smell of chicken soup on the stove and roasting chicken in the oven, the taste of her unmatchable meat *knishes,* and *kasha* dripping with melted chicken fat. I remember the family gathered around the huge dining room table on Shabbat or on holidays, with me and my cousins mixing the flavors of soda pop in our glasses.

All these memories form a delicious and sizable part of my Jewish heritage. Most of all, I remember the importance of family Bubbe instilled in me both directly and indirectly by her own example, and by the values she nurtured in my father which my father passed on to me.

Bubbe wasn't Jewish just by virtue of the fact that she was observant, belonged to a synagogue, and was raising a Jewish family, although all of those were true. Her Jewishness was who she was—as much a fact of her existence as her hair, eyes, or skin. She simply was, and the role model she created is with me still, even though she is not.

Now I am the Bubbe, living in the same city in which I grew up with my grandmother. Like her I have six children (three by birth, three by marriage to my own) and a wonderful husband with whom I share my life. I love my husband, children, and grandchildren with an intensity (although not a style) that matches hers. And like her I am Jewish—all the time, inside out, to-the-very-core-of-my-being, Jewish.

Very much unlike Bubbe, however, I am an integral part of the greater society in which I live, which is not exclusively Jewish. I have many interests outside my home and family. And I have chosen to share those interests with others beyond my intimate circle.

Neither this book nor my need to write it would have made much sense to my grandmother. She would not have understood the assimilation or intermarriage that make it relevant. She assumed that all Jews already know all about things Jewish, and that anyone who wasn't Jewish simply wouldn't want to know. In her day, that may have been true. Today, however, it's not. All Jews do not already know about things Jewish, and people who are not Jewish do want to know.

Current statistics tell us that more than half of American Jews getting married today wed spouses not born to

Judaism. *Welcome to the Family* was written for the non-Jewish part of those statistics and for their families, who may be unfamiliar with the Jewish experience.

Maybe one of the following describes you: You are *not* Jewish and . . .

- Your Jewish co-worker has just become a new father. With great joy, he invites you to join his family for the circumcision, the actual circumcision, of his newborn son. You think to yourself, *He's got to be kidding. What's this all about?*

- Your daughter has become engaged to a Jewish man, and informs you that not only are they going to have a traditional Jewish wedding in a synagogue, but that she is going to convert to Judaism. *What does that mean for her and for your precious relationship with her?*

- You have just invited your new Jewish neighbors over for an informal, spur-of-the-moment barbecue. They tell you they would love to come, but they have certain food restrictions because they keep kosher. *You haven't a clue what that means. What are you supposed to do now?*

- Your sister's Jewish father-in-law just died. Not only does she expect you to come to the funeral, she wants you to come to her in-laws' house while the family gathers. *What is expected of you? What should you bring?*

- It is Christmas. *Should you invite your Jewish friends or your extended family to your celebration?*

Or maybe the following scenario makes even more sense: you are Jewish and . . .

- One of your non-Jewish friends keeps asking you questions about Judaism that you don't know how to answer. *How do you find the answers for your friend and, even more important, for yourself?*

These scenarios are real. All have happened to people I know and countless others whom I don't. Situations like these produce uncertainty and often are fraught with anxiety. We want to do the right thing and not offend our new in-laws, our family or our friends whose customs are unfamiliar.

Let's start with a few pointers that may help your understanding as you read:

- The Judaism I describe refers predominantly to contemporary Judaism found in the United States.

- The Jewish community is commonly divided into two geographically based ancestries: *Askenazi Jews,* whose ancestors came from Eastern Europe, and *Sephardi Jews,* whose ancestors came from Spain and the southern Mediterranean.

- Whenever historical dates are used, they are followed by the letters B.C.E., meaning *before the common era,* or C.E., meaning the *common era.* Jews commonly do not use the Christian terms B.C. or A.D., which are comparable time periods to B.C.E. and C.E.

- Similarly, what Jews call the *Bible* refers loosely to those books Christians call the Old Testament. That which

Christians refer to as the New Testament is *not* part of Jewish scripture.

- I have used both he and she throughout the book in an attempt to be gender-sensitive.

- I have tried to present Jewish beliefs and practices as objectively and honestly as I can, based on my own knowledge and research. It should be noted, however, that many things described herein are my own viewpoints not definitive, authoritative facts.

CHAPTER 1

Welcome to The Family

S HORTLY AFTER OUR SON'S FIANCÉ TRACEY EM-
braced Judaism, our son Jordan called to tell me Tracey
was anxious about the upcoming High Holy Days which she
would be celebrating for the first time. She didn't know
what to expect or what was expected of her. He asked me to
talk with her about it. So one afternoon, Tracey and I went
for a drive, parked the car, and had a long talk about the
holidays and how she was feeling about them.

I told her about the service and what to expect. I sug-
gested she ask Jordan to put the service on tape and anno-
tate a prayer book. That way she could practice listening
to the tape and following the text in the prayer book, so
when the time came, she would know how to follow the
service. Just talking about it seemed to make her feel better. But as we finished our conversation, she said to me, "I
don't want to make you feel badly, but it would have been

easier if I had married into another family, one that wasn't so visible in the Jewish community."

I quickly explained to her that this visible Jewish woman knew how she felt. She was looking at me as I am now, not as I was when I was her age. It wasn't easy for me then either.

I remember, when we were in college, going for the first time to services in a Conservative synagogue with Arden, my "someday-in-the-future-husband-to-be." My upbringing had been in the Reform tradition, and I wasn't familiar with the customs of this more traditional service. I remember pulling on Arden's coat to encourage him to sit down when others did during the Amidah prayer, not knowing that the custom was to sit only when one had completed reading the prayer. I didn't know when I was supposed to stand or sit. The tunes they used for prayers weren't familiar to me. I felt like a novice, like everyone was watching me, and I didn't like it.

My discussion with Tracey about the holidays ended with a shopping spree to buy something she would enjoy wearing to the synagogue for the holidays. Needless to say she was terrific and like the rest of us, she continues to grow and learn, both Jewishly and otherwise.

Being comfortable as a Jewish adult both in the synagogue and in the community doesn't happen overnight. I know. I'm still working at it. (Two years ago I started taking Hebrew lessons.) On my desk, I have a framed greeting card, with a little stick figure doing cartwheels in a field of flowers. The caption reads, "I am in the process." I believe it!

Perhaps the most important thing you should know

about joining the Jewish family is that it is not a quick and easy process. I think that holds true whether you are joining through marriage or conversion or you're returning to the fold to reclaim your Jewish heritage. The process is often complicated by the fact that everyone has an opinion on the subject, and usually is not hesitant to express it! These strong opinions can make things difficult for those joining the Jewish family, and for their families as well.

As with all families, the Jewish family has its own rules, jokes, acceptable behaviors, unacceptable behaviors, and its own particular history. You can read this book and others like it to get the basic information about being Jewish and Judaism, but the nuances, the "rules," the humor, the collective memories, the sense of belonging, the reason certain responses are the norm to specific circumstances—all of these combine to make up the Jewish psyche. This aspect of the Jewish experience is often hard to understand and even harder to acquire. As a result, it often takes newcomers a long time *not* to feel like outsiders. Unfortunately, it often takes a long time for some Jewish people not to see newcomers that way as well.

Why? Why do Jews sometimes respond this way? What makes up the Jewish experience?

Part of the answer lies in a long history of persecution during which countless Jews were martyred, often with the blessing and encouragement of established religions, culminating in modern times with the ultimate horror of the Holocaust. Part of the answer lies in the isolation imposed by the societies in which Jews lived before coming to North America, societies in which they were ostracized, required to live together in ghettos, not allowed to interact fully with their neighbors, and limited in their opportunities for education and employment. Part of what makes up the Jewish psyche lies in the role given to "community" in the Jewish experience. Certainly for Jews in North America, part lies in the immigrant experience: leaving the "old country" to live free of life-threatening persecution, the pain of leaving families behind, the early years of sweat shops and push carts and tenement living. Another part of the answer lies in being a minority in a majority society—a minority subject to quotas, denial of career choice, and restricted neighborhoods.

And finally, Jews respond differently because *Jews are different*: Our beliefs are different, our eating habits are different, our language of prayer is different, our customs and holidays are different, even our appearance can be different. All of these factors go together to make up the Jewish psyche. The memories of the past and the fear that the events of the past will recur are a critical part of the Jewish psyche, too. That fear and those memories cannot be overlooked or minimized in understanding the Jewish experience. They constitute an integral part of who we are as Jews. Fortunately, that part is not as much of us as it once was. Today, thankfully, we concentrate more on the "*joys* of being Jewish than the *oys* of being Jewish."

For most of Jewish history, one of the rules was that Jews did not marry outside the faith. In early times, it simply was not an option; in most cities civil law did not apply to Jews who were considered second class citizens. Therefore, civil wedding ceremonies were quite rare. Jewish law prohibited marriage between Jews and non-Jews, so intermarriage wedding ceremonies could not be performed by a rabbi. It simply was not permitted. Therefore, one could not have a Jewish wedding and be part of the Jewish community. Living outside the Jewish community as a Jew was not an option, either. Thus, intermarriage was uncommon, much as it was portrayed in *Fiddler on the Roof.*

In the last few centuries, there were occasions when intermarriage did occur. If one chose to break with tradition and intermarry, however, there were consequences—in some cases severe. It was not uncommon for the family to simply cut the offending child out of their lives. Some families treated the child who had intermarried as if she had died performing the Jewish mourning rituals, the mourners prayer, and no longer having any contact with the child. Thankfully, that is no longer the case, with the possible exception of extremely orthodox families.

Today, intermarriage in North America is quite common: In fact more than half of American Jews marrying today wed people who were not born to Judaism. While no longer forbidden in the same way, intermarriage can still result in conflict for both sets of parents. In addition to all the unknowns, they may also feel rejection and betrayal by their children's choices.

For Jewish parents, the news that a child is going to marry someone not Jewish often brings out the "Jewish psyche" described above, and may not be easily accepted. Many Jewish parents and grandparents feel pain, sadness, and loss at what they consider a rejection of their heritage. They have concern for whether that heritage will be passed on to their grandchildren. They fear for the rejection of their child or his people by the family into which he is marrying. They are acutely conscious of the price paid by their ancestors simply for being Jewish, and this plays into their feelings as well.

For non-Jewish parents, the news can be equally disturbing. Being "Jewishly connected" usually is not what they expected for their children. They are concerned about what their child is getting into, and whether they will be able to celebrate Christmas and Easter with their grandchildren. They are anxious about where they fit into the picture, and they may be fearful for their child's spiritual future.

As the mother of children who chose mates *not* born to Judaism, I am blessed with the living example of a family who has been able to deal with intermarriage in a positive way. I would not be honest if I didn't admit that my hope for my children, and probably my expectation, given the "Jewishness" of our family, was that they would marry people who were Jewish. The hope that they would have Jewish mates came from all the reasons listed above, and because second only to the love in our family, the richest part of my husband's and my marriage and home life has been our shared Jewish heritage and our daily expression of that heritage through prayer and observance. I wanted that for my children as well.

But I am here to tell you that a child's intermarriage (or marriage with one who has converted to Judaism) does not have to bring pain or loss for Jewish or non-Jewish parents— adjustments in thinking perhaps, but not pain or loss. Intermarriage *does not necessarily mean* a rejection of heritage. It *does not necessarily mean* that the grandchildren cannot be part of their parents' and grandparents' heritage even while celebrating the holidays of their other grandparents as well. It *does not necessarily mean* that customs and traditions are lost.

It is with joy that I can affirm that Jewish practices are alive and well in my children's homes. It is certainly true that they are not "doing Jewish" the way we did it. But it is also true that the way we did it is not the way our parents or grandparents did it, either. In my view, neither way is right or wrong. By the same token, I hope my children's in-laws would attest that *their* values and heritage are respected and valued as well.

The Jewish family is diverse and complex, and the spectrum of identification and observance ranges from the liberal to the observant, from the religiously identified to the organizationally identified, to the ethnically identified, to those whom *others* identify as Jewish, and all the varying degrees along the way. One of the most precious qualities of the Jewish family is that any and *all of these identifications are viable* ones.

CHAPTER 2

Judaism, Jewishness, and The Jewish Experience

"A JEW IS SOMEONE WHOM ANYONE ELSE THINKS IS A Jew." At least that is one definition. Case in point: My rabbi once told about a Jewish woman who converted to Catholicism and became a nun. She was referred to by many as the Jewish nun.

In a July 1995 issue of *The New York Times*, William Safire says the following about Jewishness:

> Jewishness ain't chicken soup or Israeli politics or affection for guilt. Jewish identity is rooted in a distinctive old religion that builds character and group loyalty through close family life. That is how the Jewish people have survived through five millennia and is the light the Jews must continue to offer the world.

Welcome to the Family!

Many Jews would agree with William Safire that it is the *religion* which has kept the Jewish experience alive for the Jewish people: The religion and the character and group loyalty which comes from it. However, many would say that "chicken soup, Israeli politics, and guilt" are also a part of what it means to be Jewish. While these may not be what has kept the Jewish experience alive, certainly they are a part of what it means to be Jewish in America today.

Judaism, the "distinctive old religion" to which Safire refers, provides the foundation of Jewish living for Jews. It has at its central core the belief in one God, without human form. A religion which sees human beings as inherently good by nature, Judaism believes in a God of love. It is a faith heavily based on *moral values* with both the responsibility and the free will of individuals to choose between good and evil.

The foundation of Judaism can be found in the Torah, the first five books of the Hebrew Bible, and in all of Jewish learning past and present. Judaism is a religion which has been and continues to be nourished by an interpretive tradition, challenging, questioning, interpreting and reinterpreting the thoughts and words in the Torah. At the same time, Judaism commands both observance of rituals and ethical behaviors like living by the Ten Commandments, observing the Shabbat, the holidays, and the dietary laws, taking care of the widow, the orphan, the poor, and caring about a righteous and just way of living. It places great importance on the family, the role of the home, and study.

Holiness, *Kedusha*, is the goal which is sought through

the individual's relationship to all things: to other human beings by caring for one another and treating others the ways we would like to be treated, to the natural world and the universe by promoting environmental concerns and caring about the future of our land, to all of God's creatures by treating animals humanely, and most of all in our personal relationship with God.[1]

In addition to the religion itself, "Jewishness" is a complex combination of community, peoplehood, culture ethnicity, home, and family, all of them connected and interrelated with Judaism—the religion—as the foundation. Together, or even when taken in part, this forms the Jewish experience for contemporary Jews.

While not a race, Jews are clearly a *people*, and they are conscious of that peoplehood. They are conscious of it historically as they relate to events in the Jewish past, most dramatically the Holocaust in this century. They are conscious of it when reading the newspaper, checking for Jewish names among the stories; in social interactions, where their Jewish background can still raise barriers or comments; when experiencing or hearing about anti-Semitism, which touches the inner core. Jews are especially conscious of their peoplehood when Jews are in trouble, and that consciousness is a tie that binds, often with the result of taking action on other Jews' behalf. When war broke out in Israel in 1967, Jews who had not identified themselves as Jews in many years stepped forward to join hands with Israeli Jews to give support of all kinds. Young people dropped everything to go to Israel to help out in non-military roles. Someone I know mortgaged her home so she could send money to Israel.

Finally, Jewishness includes a *culture* and a sense of *ethnicity.* Paramount in the cultural mix is food. I can't imagine my "Jewishness" without chicken soup and *matzah* balls, *blintzes, kugle,* and *kasha.*

The others parts in the cultural mix include:

- *Language,* both Hebrew, (the language of prayer and the spoken language of the country of Israel) and Yiddish (the language of the vernacular). (*Oy vey*!, *meshugah, chutzpah,* come to mind.)

- A particular kind of *humor,* the kind that allows us to make fun of ourselves, and our immigrant experience, and sometimes the black humor of our history.

- *Customs,* such as lighting candles and eating *Challah* (egg bread) on Shabbat, and spitting and saying "pooh, pooh, pooh" to ward off the evil eye. (One of my favorites.)

- A passion for *knowledge and learning*

- *Music,* both the music of liturgy and music of the soul, the music of a culture.

- And finally, a *country,* a land of our own, the land of *Israel.*

Mordecai Kaplan, the founder of the Reconstructionist Movement of Judaism, believed that all descriptions and practices of being Jewish could fit into one of three basic categories: believing, behaving, and belonging. According to him, one could be Jewish by accepting and observing *only one* of these categories and rejecting the others, by accepting *two* and rejecting the third, or by accepting and observing all *three.* I think most Jews would agree with this interpretation. This is an important concept for those who are not Jewish to understand, because the range of practice, observance, and identity is so varied for Jews. According to this theory, whether one identifies Jewishly by belief, behavior, or a sense of belonging—or all three—one is Jewish. In this way, Judaism is far different from most other religions. Regardless of what one believes, about God, the Torah, or Judaism itself, one can still be Jewish.

BELIEVING:
WHAT JEWS BELIEVE ABOUT GOD

"In the beginning God" These are the first words in the Bible. Forever, thereafter, God is a given for religious Jews, an assumption of faith for all time.

Religious Jews typically do not spend time talking about God or focusing on belief. Rather, their faith in God is practiced by living as righteous persons by the ethical behavior God expects of them, and by fulfilling religious expectations listed in the Bible: living according to the Ten Commandments; observing the dietary laws, caring for the sick, the poor, the widowed, and the orphan; and treating other people with compassion and justice.

Judaism is a religion whose focus is on *doing* rather than on *believing,* on performance of *mitzvot* (commandments), rather than on faith. In fact, if you were to select a variety of books devoted to Judaism and looked in the table of contents to find a chapter on God or theology, you would find that many of them don't have a full chapter devoted to the subject. To my surprise, when I first began working with the Introduction to Judaism class taught by the rabbis of my community, there were twenty one lectures given on different topics—not one of them devoted to God or theology. The assumption for those planning the curriculum is that theology is included *intrinsically in everything and anything having to do with Judaism*—that the inclusion is both understood and obvious. (The students felt, by the way, that there needed to be a single lecture devoted to God to explain that fact, which the course now has.)

What do Jews believe about God? There is no single answer to that question. Some Jews believe one thing, some Jews another, and each group brings a little different twist to the basic beliefs.

Basic to *all* Jewish belief about God, however, and perhaps the most universally held belief in all aspects of Judaism is that of monotheism: the belief in one God, and only one. The *shema*, the central prayer of Judaism (sometimes referred to as the "watchword of our faith"), reaffirms this belief. Observant Jews recite it twice daily. It translates:

Hear O Israel [meaning the peoplehood of Israel, not the country],
The Lord our God,
The Lord is one.

In addition to the monotheistic concept of God, there are other theological beliefs that most religious Jews share to some degree:

A belief in a God *without human form*
A belief in God the Creator
A belief in the God of the covenant

A belief that the God to whom they pray is the God of
their ancestors

A belief that God gives them both the responsibility and
the free will to choose good or evil

A belief in a God who cares about human beings and
requires ethical behavior

A belief in a kind and loving God

Having said all this, it should be understood that God
is both *"implicit* and *explicit"* throughout Judaism and in all
of Jewish observance, thought, and practice. It is God to
whom Jews give thanks, render praise, make a blessing. It is
God to whom they acknowledge the birth of a child, the
beauty of a sunset, the sweet smell of spring. It is God to
whom they turn for solace when they are in pain or sorrow.

BEHAVING: THE OBSERVANCE OF *MITZVOT*

Being a sentimental person, I am often moved to tears. I
remember one night when Jordan was little, we were sitting at the dinner table and he said to me, "Is this a happy
cry or a sad cry?"

So, you can imagine how I responded to the births of
my grandchildren. I speak of grandchildren rather than my
own children because at the vantage point of a Bubbe, one
is not responsible for the upbringing of the precious child
or overwhelmed with all that comes with a newborn.

When a Jewish baby is born, she is given a three-fold
blessing in the hope that three things will come to her:
Torah (Jewish learning), *chuppah* (the joy of the marriage
canopy), and *ma'asim tovim* (the doing of good deeds).
The doing of good deeds is one way of defining the obser-

vance of mitzvot. The observance of mitzvot is not simply one of the most important parts of Judaism; *the observance of mitzvot is Judaism.*

The word *mitzvot* is sometimes used to mean the doing of a good deed, as in, "She did a mitzvah (singular) by taking her friend to the doctor." There are 613 mitzvot in the Torah, and Judaism places great emphasis on the performance of these good deeds. Because of this, Judaism has been described by some as a religion of deed rather than creed. The religion's primary focus in everyday life is on doing, and on living a life motivated by ethical behavior.

The mitzvah of righteous giving, known as *tzedakah*, is one of the most important concepts in Judaism, one that all Jews are expected to practice. The word literally means righteousness. Jews who make charitable contributions call it tzedakah, not charity, thus the term "righteous giving." This is a particularly meaningful part of the Jewish experience. Jewish tradition teaches that righteous giving is a part of Judaism from which no one is exempt, not even the poor. People are expected to give at their capacity, and the giving of physical support—the gift of running errands, offering a ride, or baby sitting is just as important as the gift of money.

The best way to give tzedakah is such that neither the giver nor the receiver is aware of the other. Many Jewish organizations make this possible by serving an intermediary role between those individuals who give and those who receive. In all these ways, taking care of those in need is an integral part of Jewish life. Many Jewish homes still have a tzedakah box to collect coins for giving "charity," an act often performed every week just before lighting Shabbat candles. Jews in North America contribute large sums of money to Jewish causes both here and in Israel and to other humanitarian causes as well.

Tzedakah is one way to help with the job of restoring or repairing the world, or *tikkun olam*. These words mean the perfection of the world. Tikkun olam is considered an obligation for Jews, a way to work toward perfecting creation by doing mitzvot. This is the ultimate way to observe God's commandments.

BELONGING: THE ROLE OF COMMUNITY

No matter where Jews live in the world today, it is rare to find simply individual Jews, and to Jews, any community begins with family. Traditional Judaism is primarily practiced in the *home,* and it is the *family* that is the primary institution for this practice. For instance, as our children grew up, it was at home that we observed the dietary laws, studied the children's Bible together, celebrated Shabbat on Friday nights. It was at home (and in the car) that we sang Jewish songs, listened to Jewish music, had discussions surrounding our tradition, its holidays, and its customs. It was at home that our children learned to say the blessings before and after dinner, the prayers said together at bedtime. In these ways, the roles of home and family become paramount to religious practice.

Wherever Jews are, they join their family units with other Jewish families to form a "community," no matter how loosely structured, how large or small, that community may be. A community may be a group of Jewish families celebrating holidays together, a synagogue, a Jewish school, a Jewish home for the aged . . . or the Jewish Family and Child Service. People may participate simply by playing basketball at the Jewish community center, burying their dear ones in a Jewish cemetery, or fundraising for Jewish causes.

With regard to religious observance, community is crucial, as many Jewish prayers cannot be said in solitude, but must be said in the presence of a community quorum (often called a *minyan*). For this purpose, a minyan is defined by the Orthodox as ten adult Jewish males; for Conservative and Reform it is ten Jewish adults. Adulthood is defined as after the age of *bar* or *bat mitzvah*, thirteen years for boys, twelve for girls.

In cities with large Jewish populations, the community is often very structured, usually in three major ways: religiously, with social service agencies, and organizationally. The community's *religious structure* includes synagogues of different sizes, representing different religious movements, and offering different styles of worship, often with their own religious schools, gift shops, libraries, and cemeteries.

The *social service structure* may include a Jewish Federation (the social planning, fundraising, and coordinating body of the community), a community center, a home for the aged, a Jewish family and child Service, educational facilities offering Hebrew instruction and perhaps day school, a *mikveh* (ritual bath), a kosher market with a person qualified to perform kosher ritual slaughter, a *mohel* (one who performs ritual circumcision), and Jewish book stores. Historically, Jews were not accepted in secular society and of necessity had to take care of their own. Their acceptance in Colonial America was dependent upon that premise. When the Jewish communities of Europe wrote to the governor of New Amsterdam, Peter Stuyvesant, to seek permission to settle there, permission was granted only on the condition that they would be responsible for their own. Historically then, Jewish communities have in fact taken care of their own communal needs. They still do so today. The community's *organizational structure* includes a variety of national organizations with local chapters from organizations in support of Israel and organizations concerned with social issues and concerns to local groups of various sizes and purposes usually serving social needs.

An important part of practicing Judaism is involvement in the community; "identifying Jewishly" is dependent upon it. According to Jewish tradition, one is told, "Separate not thyself from thy community."[2] The most obvious and important way to serve community is by giving one's time and resources for the betterment of society, both Jewish and beyond.

NOTES

[1] Much of this definition of Judaism was taken from a lecture by Rabbi Emanuel Rose, Portland, Oregon.

[2] From *The Sayings of the Fathers,* religious writings of wisdom.

CHAPTER 3

Understanding the Basics

A WELL KNOWN STORY IN Jewish tradition tells of a non-Jew who came to Hillel (a great rabbi and sage) and asked him to explain all of Judaism while standing on one foot. Hillel's reply was, "What is hateful unto you, do not do unto your neighbor. The rest is commentary—now go and study." Very often when this story is told, only the first part of the quotation is given. In fact, it is the second half of the message, "The rest is commentary—now go and study," that is of particular significance to Jews, because that is who we are. The devotion to study is why Jews are called the People of the Book. Learning, and the love of learning, is integral to the Jewish experience. We are still studying, asking questions, interpreting, reinterpreting, and writing commentary.

Some of the basic tenets of Jewish expression, practice, and structure are outlined in the following pages in the different approaches to Judaism.

DIFFERENT APPROACHES TO JUDAISM

The interpretation and observance in the individual expression of Jewish practice cover a wide spectrum, ranging from a cultural or ethnic identity to a deeply religious one, with everything in between. My own children demonstrate this spectrum. One has an intermarried home where Judaism is practiced by both partners with the observance of some Jewish customs and traditions. Another's intermarried home is one where Judaism is similarly practiced by both partners, and by synagogue membership and more active participation by the Jewish partner. A third has a home where one partner became Jewish as an adult, both are involved professionally in Jewish work and in synagogue participation as well.

In all three, the children of these marriages are involved in Jewish life. Their examples resemble common expressions of the contemporary Judaism found in the United States. Whether or not they are formally affiliated with a synagogue or consider themselves a part of a particular movement of Judaism, Jews today often take only those parts of the Jewish experience that are relevant to them and put the rest aside.

For example, one person might be part of a religious movement that observes Shabbat, and the sum total of that observance for her may be having fresh challah for the weekend. Another with the same affiliation may observe the Shabbat in its fullest sense of rest and renewal, participating in all of the weekly holiday rituals including synagogue worship and study, and not driving, using electricity, or using money. The same is true of holiday observance, dietary laws, and other forms of ritual. Most interpretations of Judaism leave the degree of personal observance and practice to be left to the individual.

While Judaism is only one religion, you'll find several different approaches, known as movements, in the expression of the Jewish faith. These are *not* different denominations within Judaism as in the Protestant faith. The distinctions among the three major movements—Orthodox, Reform, and Conservative—are mostly issues of practice, *not* of theology. The beliefs and rituals that unite them are far greater than those which make them different. In the United States today, most Jews who identify with any Jewish movement, do so with one of these three approaches to Judaism. In terms of their philosophic orientations, the Orthodox Movement lies at one end of the spectrum focusing on authenticity and strictly following Jewish law; the Reform Movement is at the other end of the spectrum, focusing on relevance and placing emphasis on social justice and ethics; and the Conservative Movement lies somewhere in between, following Jewish law, but allowing for contemporary interpretation and change.

I should also mention a smaller group founded in twentieth-century America. The Reconstructionist Movement, defines itself as "The evolving religious civilization of the Jewish People." The movement's "diverse views of God share an emphasis on godliness rather than on the supernatural," a major difference in the way in which God traditionally has been viewed in Judaism.

ORTHODOX JUDAISM

Orthodox Judaism is the all encompassing, "traditional" approach to Judaism most similar to that practiced by the Jews before modern times. Its followers are considered to be the most observant. Orthodox Jews interpret the Torah as having come directly from God, and believe that faith-

Rabbi Zevi Yehuda Hakohen Kook [1891-1982], a revered rabbi, scholar, and mystic of the Orthodox tradition.

ful Jews *must follow* God's laws and mitzvot not simply as options, but as requirements. Orthodox Jews, therefore, strictly adhere to the laws of daily life described in the Torah. For example, my maternal grandmother (my Orthodox Bubbe) *davened* (prayed) the daily service every morning and night of her life. She learned this service as a child in the old country by standing outside the room where her brothers were being taught, as in those days women were not given Hebrew instruction. She also strictly observed the Shabbat, not cooking, using electricity, working in any way, or riding in a car. She followed the dietary laws of the Torah to the letter. Once, when she was in her seventies, she took a nine hour plane trip from her home in Michigan to Portland, Oregon. She refused to eat a bite of food on her journey because the airline had forgotten to bring kosher food.

Even Orthodox Judaism, however, encompasses a wide range of practice. At one extreme are the ultra-Orthodox, sometimes known as Hasidim, who often live in insular communities and, in everything from wardrobe to diet, lead lives much like those of Jews living centuries ago in Eastern Europe. Even in Israel, in a climate much warmer than that of Eastern Europe, these Jews still wear heavy, long black coats, long pants, and hats often trimmed in fur.

At the other extreme are the Modern Orthodox, who adhere strictly to the mitzvot—including *kashrut* (the Jewish dietary laws) and the observance of Shabbat—but who are much more engaged in mainstream society. While the ultra-Orthodox tend to be educated only at *yeshivoth* (schools of Jewish learning), many Modern Orthodox men and women pursue education at the same colleges and universities as other American students. Although Orthodox Judaism dictates specific religious roles for men and women—the women's role being reserved for maintaining the home and raising the children—many modern Orthodox women are professionals and even consider themselves feminists.

Religious worship services in Orthodox synagogues are

conducted almost entirely in Hebrew, and men and women are seated separately. The synagogue is considered the domain of the man, and women are not counted in a minyan (the quorum of ten adults needed for some prayers) or permitted to lead or participate in certain rituals of the service. The home is considered the domain of the woman, and her role as wife and mother is greatly respected.

REFORM JUDAISM

Reform Judaism, which began in nineteenth century Germany, was an early organized response of Jews to the modern world. Its creation was an attempt to help Jews bridge the gap between their new found civil status as citizens and their desire to hold onto their Jewish heritage. The Reform

Women and men are given equal status in all forms of synagogue worship in the Reform tradition. Here Rabbi Laurie Rutenberg blows the shofar, ram's horn, for the holiday of Rosh Hashana.

Movement chose to de-emphasize the rituals separating Jews from Gentiles, particularly those perceived as no longer relevant. Instead, the Reform Movement emphasized the ethical ideals of the Bible, particularly the writings of the Prophets. Reform Judaism does not believe that every word in the Torah and its commentaries comes directly from God. It emphasizes ethical behavior and social action as primary to its agenda. While considered the most liberal of the movements in Judaism, Reform Jews are committed to Jewish tradition. They interpret that tradition as a matter of individual and informed choice.

Services in Reform synagogues are conducted in English as well as Hebrew. Men and women are given equal status in all forms of worship and synagogue involvement.

CONSERVATIVE JUDAISM

Conservative Judaism established a rabbinical school in New York City—which still exists today—in 1887, emerging as a movement shortly thereafter. It began to provide a modern but more traditional alternative to Reform Judaism. The Conservative Movement is considered by some to be the moderate version of Judaism, retaining much from tradition and mitzvot, yet offering a more liberal approach than the Orthodox. The Conservative Movement believes the Torah was divinely inspired, and that Jewish law has evolved over the course of time and is still evolving. For instance, the role of women has changed dramatically in my own lifetime. Women are not only counted in the minyan, permitted to be called to the Torah to give blessings and read from the Torah, they may also be ordained as rabbis and cantors. As a movement, Conservative Judaism emphasizes the observance of Shabbat, the dietary laws, ethical living, and daily ritual. Conservative Jews present a wide range in the practice of these standards.

Religious worship services in Conservative synagogues are quite traditional, using more Hebrew than English. Both men and women may take advantage of all educational opportunities, including preparation for both bar and bat mitzvah, but the decision as to whether women fully participate in the Torah service or are counted in the minyan is still made by each individual synagogue.

THE TORAH: THE SOURCE

The Torah is the most sacred object in Jewish life, as it contains the writings most sacred to Judaism. The Torah is the Jewish scroll of the law that consists of the first five books of the Bible: Genesis, Exodus, Leviticus, Numbers, and Deuteronomy. It is the source for everything Jewish: recorded early history, from the creation of Adam and Eve to the coming to the promised land; Jewish law, from the dietary laws to the Ten Commandments; and ethical behavior, from how to do business to caring for the poor.

The Torah's presence is treated with great reverence and ceremony. We show our respect by how we hold, drape, read and even carry these ancient scrolls. The Torah is housed in the synagogue in a decorated cabinet known as the *aron kodesh* (holy ark). The ark is created especially for holding and honoring the Torah, and it is always placed front and center in the synagogue. Usually, this is found on the eastern wall of synagogues in America, so that worshipers face Jerusalem during prayers.

Each Torah scroll is covered with a beautiful decorative covering called a mantle. In addition, the Torah often is adorned with beautiful silver fittings. Often these decorations are given by members of the congregation in honor or in memory of someone, and are so inscribed. Common decorations include a crown, bells, special ornaments placed on the rollers around which the scroll is wrapped, a *yad* (pointer) hung by a chain like a necklace, or a decorative hanging placed over the front portion called a breast plate. The Sephardic custom is to encase the Torah in an ornately detailed, boxlike covering, also quite beautiful. Most synagogues have more than one Torah scroll; some have many.

The Torah is handwritten in Hebrew on parchment made from animal skin by someone called a *sofer* (scribe). (The laws surrounding the writing of the scrolls are so involved that a sofer must be ritually trained and prepared before even placing ink to parchment.) The parchment is written in single segments which are arduously and lovingly sewn together to form a large scroll, which then is wrapped around two wooden rollers. If one were to completely unroll a Torah (which we do in our synagogue on the holiday of Simchat Torah) it would be 100-150 feet for an average size Torah.

When the ark is opened and the Torah becomes visible, the entire congregation stands as a sign of respect. When it is removed from the ark, it is often carried through the aisles of the synagogue so people may touch it. Congregants touch the Torah cover with the edge of their prayer shawl (*tallit*) or their prayer book, or hand and then kiss whatever has touched the Torah. They remain standing until the Torah is placed on the reader's table. At

Reading the Torah scrolls during a bar mitzvah.

the conclusion of the Torah reading, the scrolls usually are carried around the synagogue again before being returned to the ark.

The Torah is read, portion by portion, every Shabbat during the year so that in the course of a year the entire scroll is read. Thus, in any given week, in any synagogue throughout the world, a part of the same portion is chanted. The weekly portion, is referred to as the *sedra* (order) or *parashah* (portion) of the week. Some synagogues use a triennial cycle, thereby reading only one third of the portion each week, so that the reading of the entire Torah is completed only once in a three-year period; some simply read the beginning section of the portion. These customs belong to specific synagogues, and probably originated because the services took too long for congregants if the entire portion was read.

While the word *Torah* is most often used to refer to the handwritten scroll of Jewish law found in the synagogue, in its broader sense Torah means learning or study. It also can refer to the totality of Jewish writings, which includes not only the *Pentateuch* (the first five books of the Bible), but the whole Hebrew Bible and the body of commentaries, teachings, Jewish writings, and recorded oral discussions that make up Jewish learning. The most noted source of commentaries is the Talmud, which is the authoritative body of Jewish tradition. Edited in stages and concluded in about 500 C.E., the Talmud contains the written legal and ethical discussions of the rabbis whose interpretations of the Pentateuch were known as the oral law.

It takes a special skill to be able to read directly from the Torah scroll. Written Hebrew typically has special symbols to indicate vowels, but the Hebrew written in the Torah has neither vowels nor punctuation. In addition, when the Torah is read, it is chanted to a special trope (or tune) which is used only for that purpose. The musical notes designated for Torah reading also do not appear in the scroll itself. The Torah is so precious that, when it is read, a yad, is used to follow the text so the parchment is not actually touched by the reader.

THE COVENANT

In the book of Genesis, God spoke to Abraham saying, "I will establish My covenant between Me and you, and I will make you . . . . the father of a multitude of nations . . . . Such shall be the covenant between Me and you and your offspring to come . . . every male among you shall be circumcised . . . and that shall be the sign of the covenant."

God established an agreement with Abraham and his descendents for all time, in which the Jews are to keep God's laws. In return God promised them the land of Canaan and agreed to watch over them and be their God. Later in the Bible, God entered into another covenant, with Moses at Mt. Sinai, with the giving and the acceptance of the Ten Commandments and the laws which followed.

A covenant was established between God and Israel, the Jewish people, in Exodus 6:7: "I will take you to be My people, and I will be your God." This statement marked the beginning of the relationship between God and the Jews as a people. God establishes a relationship to which Jews are wed to this day. Jewish males still bear the sign of the covenant through circumcision on the eighth day after birth, and parents of Jewish baby girls more and more frequently are combining covenant ceremonies with their baby naming. As a people, all branches of Judaism observe the covenant through the obligation of tikkun olam, the completion of creation by helping to achieve the perfection of the world.

SHABBAT

Shabbat (or the Sabbath) is basic to the Jewish experience. It's my favorite, and I often tell the students in the Introduction to Judaism class that it is our best asset, a holiday that comes every single week to remind us of who we are, and, more important, who we can be. When the sun sets on Friday, all the trivial details of the work week disappear.

Welcome to the Family!

The phone doesn't ring, schedules don't have to be met, and the entire day is set aside for being with the ones you love.

Shabbat is simply the most special of Jewish holidays. It commemorates the fact that after God created the world, God rested on the seventh day and hallowed it as the Sabbath. Just as God rested, we are told to rest. For me, Shabbat is a weekly opportunity to step back from the business and "busy-ness" of my day-to-day world and take my time to replenish my heart, soul, and body by simply being rather than doing. It is a day for personal, individual, and spiritual renewal, which can be done at home, alone with loved ones, or in synagogue, participating in religious worship and study.

We are told in Exodus 20:8-11, "Remember the Sabbath day and keep it holy. Six days you shall labor and do all your work, but the seventh day is a Sabbath of your God: you shall not do any work. For in six days God made heaven and earth and sea, and all that is in them, and God rested on the seventh day."

Observant Jews interpret "you shall not do any work" on the Sabbath day in its literal sense. What that means in contemporary terms is that on the Sabbath one does not drive a car, strike a match, watch television, listen to the radio, use any electricity (unless it has been turned on before sundown), exchange money, carry, tear, garden, cook, or participate in any kind of business or economic enterprise. This observance of the Sabbath truly sets the day apart from the rest of the week.

Shabbat begins at sundown on Friday night. The observance of the holiday begins with the blessing and lighting of the Shabbat candles. This blessing usually is recited

Turn of the century Shabbat candleholder belonging to the author's grandmother.

by the woman of the household. After lighting candles, many families follow with a festive Sabbath dinner. This may include such foods as gefilte fish, chopped liver, chicken soup, chicken, *kugle*, (noodle pudding), and kasha. For observant families, Shabbat begins with the lighting of the candles, followed by the evening service at synagogue, and then the evening meal.

As the family sits around the Sabbath table, the celebration often begins with the singing of Shabbat songs. In my home, after we have sung a few songs, my husband reads the passage from Proverbs that describes a woman of valor. Then he blesses any of our children who are

Welcome to the Family!

Ceremonial cups used for the *kiddush* blessing over the wine.

present with the priestly blessing:

"May the Lord bless you, and keep you: May the Lord make His face to shine upon you, and be gracious unto you: May the Lord turn His face unto you, and give you peace" (Leviticus 19:1).

When our children are present, they bless their children in turn.

Before eating, the *kiddush* (blessing over the wine) is said. It is usually recited by the man of the household, who raises the kiddush cup as he recites the blessing. It is followed by the *Hamotzi*, the blessing over the bread. In this case the bread is a *challah*, which is covered with a cloth until the blessing is said. Challah is a traditional kind of bread, usually a sweet egg bread. Often there are two *challot* (pl) as a remembrance of the double portion of *manna* provided in the story of the Exodus. When the person making the blessing is ready to do so, the cover is removed, the blessing is said, and the bread is eaten and passed around to those at the table, so they may eat of it as well.

The Friday night home observance around the Shabbat table is a special time. There is nothing quite like the warmth, the feeling of peace, the sharing and joy of family that occurs at the Shabbat meal. Part of the experience is the comforting knowledge that it will be recreated every single week, at this meal where we can sit at the table for a long time, just being together. This is a key example of the importance of home and family in the observance of Jewish tradition.

Some families go to Friday night Shabbat services. In many Reform and Conservative synagogues, services on Friday evenings are held after the Shabbat meal at 8:00 or 8:15. Many synagogues celebrate the joy of the Sabbath with an *oneg shabbat* following services to which everyone attending is invited. (*Oneg* means rejoicing. An *oneg shabbat* is a little reception, tea and cookies, to celebrate the Shabbat). For many, however, the more important synagogue service takes place on Saturday morning. During that service, the weekly Torah portion is read.

The remainder of the day is spent resting, reading, studying the Torah, perhaps taking a nap or a walk, eating, and spending time with family and friends. It is also considered a double mitzvah to make love with one's partner on Shabbat.

Shabbat concludes Saturday night when three stars appear in the sky. If one cannot see three stars, it is considered dark enough for Havdalah when one holds up a blue thread

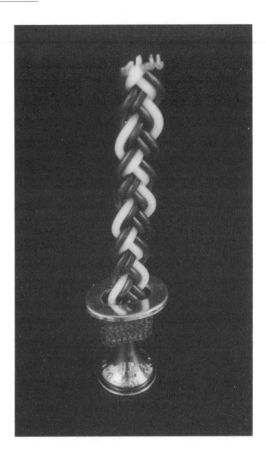

The braided
candle used in
the Havdalah
ceremony.

and a white thread and it is too dark to distinguish between
them. The religious ending of the Sabbath is observed with
a brief service called *Havdalah*, which may be done at
home. Havdalah begins with the lighting of a beautiful,
braided candle to symbolize the return of the work-a-day
week. Blessing over wine is sung, and finally sweet spices
are savored—cloves, cinnamon, and allspice—to recall the
sweetness of the Sabbath. Havdalah concludes with the
singing of a song extolling Elijah the prophet who, accord-

ing to tradition, will announce the coming of the Messiah, and a song wishing all present a good week. When the candle is blown out, or extinguished in the cup of wine, we wish one another *"Shavuah Tov!"* a good week. We always kiss everyone present as we give this greeting, and thereby let go of the Shabbat and welcome the coming week with joy and anticipation.

Observing Shabbat can involve as much or as little as one chooses. For many, religious worship in synagogue and prayer are part of the Shabbat experience. For some, study is involved as well. For others, it is not a "religious" day, but a day of rest that can simply be enjoyed, a day for self-renewal and self-expression, a day for doing what one doesn't have time to do during the week, a day to be spent with family and friends.

Some years ago when our youngest was about to leave home for college, our daughter Diana asked me, "What are you and Dad going to do for Shabbat now that we're all going to be gone?"

"I don't want to burst your bubble," I told her, "But we had Shabbat before you came, and we will have it after you've gone!"

As I spoke those words, I remembered the first Shabbat Arden and I ever celebrated as a married couple. After a week-long honeymoon, we had driven cross-country to start our lives together in an un-air-conditioned, furnished apartment in New Haven, Connecticut. We arrived, hot and tired, late on a Wednesday evening. We worked non-stop on Thursday and Friday, trying to unpack boxes, buy necessities, and turn someone else's furniture and decor into *our* home—all before the sun set on Friday. I can still see us as we stood together, hot and sweaty in this humid climate unfamiliar to us, hanging the *Mezuzah* on the doorpost of our new home, at the last possible minute on Friday evening. (A mezuzah is a decorative case housing specific prayers hung on the doorpost of a Jewish home.) When it was hung, we bathed and dressed for Shabbat. We sat down to eat long after the sun had set, but we were so very proud of ourselves! We began our blessings not only for that Shabbat celebration, but for all the ones to follow.

Shabbat is one of Judaism's great treasures, and it's certainly one of mine. It has enriched my life, and provided a safe haven and tranquil port for me and my family in what is sometimes a stormy, very busy, sea. Over the years, our observance of Shabbat has changed. It gets bigger or smaller depending on who is with us; we sometimes add new traditions and special songs and put others away, but always Shabbat is the most special day of the week.

SYNAGOGUE AND PRAYER

If you enter a synagogue anywhere in the world, some things are always the same. The style of architecture may differ; the style of prayer and music used may differ; the customs observed by the congregation may differ, but *every* synagogue, no matter what kind, will have these three things in common:

1. There will be at least one Torah,
2. There will be an ark to house the Torah, and
3. Above the ark, there will be a lamp called a *ner tamid* (eternal light). As its name implies, the ner tamid remains lit at all times to show the eternal presence of God.

Temple Beth Israel in Portland, Oregon.

The synagogue is usually built so that worshippers face the ark as they pray, and the ark is placed so that the direction they will be facing is toward Jerusalem. In North America, for example, this means that the ark will be found on the eastern wall of the sanctuary.

Many synagogues have a section on the wall with multiple listings of names, sometimes with a small electric light adjacent to each. These plaques are given in memory of loved ones who have passed on. On the anniversary of the death of a loved one—the *yahrzeit* (the date on the Jewish calendar)—the light is turned on. When it is the yahrzeit for my parents or in-laws and we go to synagogue to say the appropriate prayers, the first thing I do on entering the sanctuary is look for their names on the wall. For me, it is an affirmation of sorts, and an important one.

There are many variations in Jewish worship services in North America, probably as many as there are synagogues. The length of the service, the tunes used for chanting prayers, the inclusion or exclusion of certain prayers, the amount of Hebrew, the presence or absence of a cantor or choir, which prayer book is used—all of these things vary from synagogue to synagogue. By and large, however, services in each of the movements of Judaism are similar in style and content as others of that movement, and most things are common to all.

In our synagogue, adult males are expected to cover their heads with a *kippah* upon entering the synagogue as a sign of respect for God, and Jewish men are also expected to wear a *tallit* (prayer shawl) for the Saturday morning service. Both are available in the foyer, but many people will choose to bring their own. Increasingly in liberal congregations you may see women with a kippah or a tallit as well. Although this is a relatively new custom, it is becoming more common.

Jewish prayer is both individual and communal. Prayers are said both silently and aloud, individually and as a congregation. In more traditional synagogues, silent prayers are murmured softly rather than read silently, and upon completion of the prayer the individual is seated. Often people who are praying this way (which is called *davening* in Yiddish) sway or rock slightly back and forth as they pray. It is not unusual in some synagogues for congregants to arrive at various times for the Saturday morning service; for example, some might arrive in time for a certain part of the service, not necessarily the beginning. So if you are attending Saturday morning Sabbath services, you might want to check with someone who regularly attends services to find out the appropriate time to arrive.

Hebrew is the universal language of Jewish prayer. Most American prayer books are written in both Hebrew and English, and most synagogues use both languages as part of the service. If one is reading the prayer book in either a Conservative or Orthodox synagogue, it will open from what English readers consider the back of the book, and the pages will be numbered accordingly. This is to accommodate the Hebrew language which is read from right to left, rather than from left to right as English is read.

In addition to Hebrew prayers used as part of a structural service, individual prayers are said alone or with others in the home. In particular, prayers are often said before and after a meal. Someone asked me once what saying the blessing before and after meals meant to me. This is prayer at its most basic, thanking God for the food we are about to eat or have just eaten. I had never thought about it much since my husband and I decided when we got married that it would be a part of our home. As I reflected on it, however, it became clear that my feelings about these two prayers were much more than gratitude to God. Every time I say these prayers two things are happening for me: I am recreating myself as a Jew and I am connecting to all Jews everywhere, past and present.

If you are attending religious services in a synagogue, there are some things you'll want to know that will make the service more comfortable for you.

- It is courteous in any synagogue to stand when the ark housing the Torah is opened and to remain standing until it is closed, and when the Torah is lifted or moved. (Sometimes in Reform synagogues the ark remains open during a part of the service when the congregation may be seated. If this is the case, the rabbi normally will announce that you may be seated.)

- In Orthodox synagogues, men and women are not seated together. They are seated in sections separated by a divider or wall called a *mehitzah*, or women are seated in the balcony, if the synagogue has one.

- When prayers are said referring to Israel, in almost all cases it means the people of Israel, the Jewish people, *not* the state of Israel. If the prayer were for the country of Israel, that distinction would be made clear either by the text of the prayer itself or by the rabbi.

- There are some occasions in Orthodox and Conservative services when only some of the people stand, rather than the entire congregation. This is true when the *kaddish* (mourner's prayer) is recited, and only those in mourning or commemorating the anniversary of a loved one's death will stand. This practice also is true during the recitation of a part of the service called the *amidah*, the core prayer of silent devotion which is said standing.

- Appropriate dress for a religious service in synagogue would be what one might call street wear—what you might wear to church or to a downtown business meeting. This applies to the synagogue part of a bar/bat mitzvah, as well, and also to a funeral. Weddings and parties vary and are not a part of the religious service. If you are not sure, check with your host or hostess.

HISTORICAL PERSPECTIVE

Jews are the descendants of the ancient Hebrews of the Bible. They date the beginning of their history back to Abraham and the covenant God made with him. Abraham is considered the first Jewish person. Abraham, Isaac (his son), and Jacob (his grandson) are the patriarchs of Judaism. To this day, Jewish prayer is directed to the God of Abraham, Isaac and Jacob. Because of today's gender sensitivity, the matriarchs Sarah, Rebecca, Rachel and Leah are often included in prayer as well.

Through Moses and the giving and receiving of the Ten Commandments, the children of Israel made a second covenant with God. Their acceptance of the Ten Commandments and the laws that followed resulted in the Jewish people choosing to take on God's laws forever and God's promise to be with them always.

Jewish history *is* the history recorded in the Bible. After the conclusion of the events recorded in the Bible, however, Jewish history continued to unfold throughout the world and beyond the land of the Bible. The Jewish people adapted the customs and ceremonies of the lands and peoples which ingathered them for two millennia. Their language underwent changes, their religious practices developed, and their bonds as people of God were reforged.

Jewish history covers more than four thousand years. (Traditionally, the year 2001 is numbered 5761 on the Jewish Calendar, dating back to creation.) In the following pages you will find a timeline on some of the events in that history.

Welcome to the Family!

A Timeline

3761 B.C.E.   Creation of Adam

1812   Birth of Abraham

1428   Beginning of slavery in Egypt

1392   Birth of Moses

1312   Exodus from Egypt. The giving of the Torah at Mt. Sinai

825   First Temple completed

586   First Temple destroyed. Exile of the Jews to Babylonia begins

356   The story of the holiday of Purim

352   Second Temple completed

161   The miracle of Hanukkah

70 C.E.   Second Temple destroyed

73   Fall of Masada, the mountain top fortress where approximately a thousand Jews chose to take their own lives rather than submit to Roman rule and give up their Judaism

359   Permanent Jewish lunar calendar

1290   Expulsion of the Jews from England

1394   Expulsion of the Jews from France

1492   Expulsion of the Jews from Spain

1654   First Jewish settlement established in North America

1791   French National Assembly granted full civil rights to Jews

1815   German Jewish immigration to America began

1882   Mass immigration of Russian Jews to America begins

1894   Dreyfus trial (In France) in which a Jewish military officer was framed for treason because of anti-semitism, sent to Devil's Island, and later found innocent and exonerated

1897   First Zionist Congress (in Basel, Switzerland)

1933   Hitler comes to power in Germany

1938   Kristallnacht, the night of broken glass, when windows in Jewish stores and homes throughout Germany were broken, synagogues were burned, Jews were beaten and jailed; lack of response from anywhere in the world gave Hitler the "permission" needed to carry out the Holocaust

1938–45 The Holocaust, the orchestrated genocide of six million Jews during the Nazi regime of World War II which not only resulted in the loss of one third of the world's Jewish population, but also destroyed six thousand Jewish communities in Europe, the center of Jewish culture at that time

1948   State of Israel declared

1972   First woman rabbi ordained by the Reform Movement

1990   National Jewish Population Survey, analyzing Jewish demographics in the U.S.

WOMEN IN JUDAISM

Several years ago, as Arden and I were entering the traditional synagogue to attend an evening minyan, we were greeted enthusiastically by a gentleman who was counting each new entry in the hopes of quickly reaching the needed quorum of ten.

"Oh, good! We have one more," he exclaimed. "Here's Arden!" Under my breath I quietly responded, "And chopped liver!"

He looked at me and said, "What did you say?"

I replied that I had said, "And chopped liver."

Without missing a beat and with a little smile on his face he said, "Sorry folks. What I meant to say was, 'Here comes Lois. And she brought Arden with her.'"

I can understand and even appreciate the integrity and consistency of the Orthodox view of limited roles for women. I don't necessarily like it, and I wouldn't be comfortable calling such a synagogue home, but I understand that is the way it is *there* and I can respect that belief for those who choose to accept it. Having said that, I am grateful for the changing roles women have had over the last century in the more liberal movements of Judaism.

The opportunities for Jewish expression and practice for women are a great example of tradition, contemporary concerns, and ancient laws melding in new and wonderful ways. Now women are spreading their influence throughout Jewish culture, religion, and family, taking their place as rabbis, cantors, board presidents, creators of ritual, and scholars. As women have taken their rightful place in our society, many rituals that at one time were reserved only for men have been changed to include women. Likewise, many new rituals are available today for women making life transitions, from rituals for pregnancy or miscarriage to naming ceremonies and others honoring the joys and sorrows in women's lives.

The first bat mitzvah occurred in the United States in 1922. Prior to that time, bat mitzvah was not an option for young Jewish women. Morechai Kaplan, a noted American rabbi who had five daughters and no sons, instituted the ceremony, and his daughter Judith became the first bat

A young woman at her bat mitzvah.

mitzvah. Today it is common practice in many Reform, Conservative, and Reconstructionist synagogues. In even some traditional synagogues, a form of bat mitzvah has been adopted that is not in conflict with traditional observance.

Changes have also occurred regarding women wearing a tallit or kippah, or putting on tefillin. While these practices were once reserved for Jewish males only, they are now the option of women in the liberal movements of Judaism, and they are options being exercised in increasing numbers. It is no longer unusual to see these practices honored by women.

In the Orthodox tradition, there are some rituals and mitzvot in which women are not permitted to participate. While this used to be true in the Conservative tradition as well, today women have equal opportunities for participation in ritual, and they may be ordained as rabbis and cantors as is true in the Reform tradition.

THE JEWISH DIETARY LAWS: FROM KOSHER TO *TRAYF*

So there I was, a bride of three weeks, three thousand miles from home, in a strange city knowing almost no one, keeping house for the first time in my life, in the summer of 1960. I had little experience in grocery shopping and cooking and not a clue based on experience of how to keep a "kosher" home. I had read the right book,[1] which answered all the necessary questions, but it was overwhelming nonetheless. What things could be eaten with what other things? What packaged items were acceptable, and what were not? And just how does one know for sure?

Fortunately, I had two allies: a new friend who had been keeping a kosher home for many years, and Barney, the butcher at the kosher supermarket. My friend was only a phone call away. And what can I say about the butcher? He was a fatherly figure in his fifties or sixties who custom-cut orders for his customers, one at a time. He knew his business and would patiently take the time to explain in Yiddish accented English just what cut of meat I really wanted. As he cut and packaged my purchases, he gave me a running commentary on what to cook and how to cook it. I'm sure he never knew how important he was to my success as a homemaker. He was priceless. In addition, I learned to look for symbols on packaged goods and to read labels. What follows is some of what I learned.

The kosher food laws are designed to bring holiness to an otherwise mundane experience—that of eating. Food is considered kosher when it meets certain requirements that make it acceptable according to Jewish law. *Kashrut* is the term given to this system of laws. According to Kashrut, some foods are prohibited, some are permitted, and some require special preparations. The Hebrew word *kosher* literally means fit. Food that is not fit to eat is called *trayf.* One who adheres to Jewish dietary laws is said to "keep kosher."

Kosher food laws define

1. which animals may be eaten and which may not;
2. the methods to be used for the ritual slaughtering of those animals which may be eaten; and
3. the rules surrounding the separation of meat and dairy products, which may not be eaten at the same meal. (Meat products are defined as kosher meat and poultry. They don't include fish. Dairy products are defined as milk and dairy products made with milk, butter, or cheese. They do not include eggs.)

It's sometimes confusing to those who don't observe the laws of kashrut to know just which foods are considered kosher. Following is a list of acceptable foods according to Jewish dietary laws.

- All fruits and vegetables are considered kosher.

- Processed food products are considered kosher when they are marked with a label showing they have been approved as such. These labels, shown on the outside of a printed package, include a printed "O" with a small "u" inside, a capital "K," or the word Kosher. Sometimes these labels are accompanied by the word "Dairy" or the letter "D" to symbolize dairy; or they may use the word "pareve" or the letter "P," which means the product not only is kosher, but can be used with either meat or dairy products.

- In order for meat or poultry to be kosher, it must be ritually slaughtered and labeled as such. Animals considered acceptable for kosher slaughter are those which have a cloven hoof and chew their cud, most commonly cows and lambs. Additionally, there are some parts of the animal which are prohibited.

- Chicken, turkey, and duck are all permitted poultry.

- Only those fish with fins and scales are permitted. No shellfish of any kind is permitted.

Not all Jews observe the dietary laws, and not all those who observe them observe all of them. While both the Conservative and Orthodox movements support the observance of kashrut, it is not enforced upon congregants. Many Jews, whether or not they keep kosher, observe the restriction against eating pork. Many who observe kashrut at home do not do so when eating out. Kashrut has not been part of the Reform tradition, and it is not generally observed by Reform Jews in the traditional sense.

In our own home, we observe most of the kosher food laws. I remember the first time I had to confront the issue with one of our children.

When he was four years old, our oldest son Joel was

invited to a birthday party that included a hot dog lunch. Not only were the hot dogs *not* kosher, they were to be followed with ice cream and cake. What to do? I decided to ask the birthday boy's mom if I could provide tuna fish to go in the hot dog bun, thus removing the problem. Putting the tuna in the bun, I thought, would not call attention to Joel's being different. Of course that was fine with her.

I agonized throughout the afternoon, waiting for Joel to come home from the party. Would the other children think he was different? Would he feel badly not having a hot dog when everyone else had one? Would he eat it anyway, and then realize he couldn't have ice cream and cake? Was it fair for us to require our children to follow our rules and values?

As he walked in the door, I bombarded him with the usual questions. "How was the party?" "Did he like your present?" "Did you have fun?" "Who was there?" And finally "What did you have for lunch?" He gleefully replied, "I had potato chips for lunch!"

So much for my worries! When a similar event occurred when he was six, Joel came home from a birthday party and said, "I'm so glad we keep kosher." When I asked, "Why?", he told me it made him feel special.

I don't know if "feeling special" was the original intent of our ancestors, but it sure works for me!

NOTES

[1] *The Jewish Dietary Laws*, by Samuel Dresner, (New York: Burning Bush Press).

CHAPTER 4

Life Cycle Events
Moments in Time

L IFE CYCLE EVENTS—those moments that are the milestones of our lives—continue to live on in our memory long after they are over. They link us to the traditions of our past and send us to the future with renewed hope.

In the Jewish tradition, the life cycle events of birth, bar and bat mitzvah, weddings, death and mourning carry specific rituals, most of which have been used for centuries. For example, at a bar or bat mitzvah, the child is able to put on a tallit for the first time. His parents usually give it to him on the pulpit at the Friday evening service. The act of passing the heritage from parent to child enhances the ceremony and gives it more meaning than a simple rite of passage. The same is true at a wedding when the glass is broken. This is the last act of the wedding except for the kiss. Theoretically, the actual ceremony is over—the couple is married. The addition of this special Jewish ritual sets it apart from any other wedding. For me, these rituals are opportunities to connect again to the heritage I hold so dear.

JEWISH WEDDINGS

When our son Jordan was about to marry his newly Jewish bride, Tracey, Arden and I got together with his future in-laws a week or so before the wedding to explain some of the customs peculiar to a Jewish wedding. What follows are some of the things we shared with them.[1]

- Traditional Jewish weddings are performed by rabbis. The ceremony takes place under a *chuppah* (wedding canopy). It may take place at any time other than Shabbat (Friday night sundown until Saturday night sundown), Jewish holidays, and some designated periods on the calendar.

- The ceremony begins with words of greeting, after which the rabbi says blessings over a cup of wine shared by the bride and groom. The groom then presents the bride with a ring, which may be accompanied by the bride presenting the groom with a ring. The groom's declaration to the bride, first in Hebrew and then English, is, "Be thou consecrated unto me with this ring according to the laws of Moses and Israel." If she gives her groom a ring, the bride may make the same declaration or use one taken from the Song of Songs or some other appropriate source. The *ketubah* (wedding contract) is read, and the cantor or

A chuppah wedding canopy, made from tablecloth that will be used for the family's Shabbat celebrations.

rabbi chants the *sheva brachot* (seven blessings) in Hebrew. These blessings rejoice in creation, the relationship between humanity and God, and the happiness of the bride and groom. At some point in the ceremony, the rabbi addresses personal remarks to the couple. At the conclusion of the ceremony, the rabbi often asks the couple to receive God's blessings as a special prayer is said on their behalf. Finally the groom (and sometimes the bride) will shatter a glass vessel, wrapped in a cloth, with his (her) foot. When the glass is broken, the congregation often shouts, "Mazel Tov!"

- Bridal parties, (bridesmaids, ushers etc.) are at the option of the bride and groom, as in any other wedding.

A couple celebrates their wedding ceremony under the chuppah.

- Orthodox (and some Conservative) brides will visit the *mikveh,* (the ritual bath) in the week prior to their wedding as a special form of spiritual cleansing to prepare them for their new life transition.

- The groom, if he chooses, may be called to the Torah for a special blessing at a service preceding the wedding where the Torah is read. Most commonly this is done on the Shabbat before the wedding, but may also be done any day the Torah is read during the week before the wedding. This custom is called an *aufruf.* If the synagogue allows women to be called to the Torah, the bride and groom may be called individually or as a couple. Following the reading of the Torah portion, a special blessing is said for the couple in honor of their forthcoming marriage. As the couple returns to their seats, they often are serenaded and showered with candies in the hope that they will have a sweet life.

- Male guests, whether they are Jewish or not, are generally asked to wear kippot for the wedding ceremony if the congregation uses them.

- The chuppah under which the wedding takes place symbolizes the bridal chamber and the Jewish home the couple is about to create together. It also is symbolic of the importance of hospitality.

- Jewish brides today seldom come down the aisle to the strains of Wagner's wedding march. More and more commonly, Jewish music, often contemporary Israeli music, is used.

- Often the bride and groom walk down the aisle on the arms of both parents. Sometimes the parents stand under the chuppah with the bridal couple during the ceremony.

- The traditional ketubah is a wedding contract, a legal document designed to protect the rights of the bride and to codify the groom's obligations to her. While its language is somewhat archaic and some of the obligations do not meet contemporary standards, its original intent was to assure that the groom was financially responsible for his wife's needs and personally responsible for treating her in a kindly and humane manner. Some Reform rabbis use a modern poetic text rather than the traditional one.

- In traditional ceremonies, the ring is placed on the index finger of the right hand, this being considered the traditional ring finger and historically also the one most clearly seen by the witnesses who sign the ketubah. It is usually returned to the "ring" finger after the ceremony.

- The breaking of the glass at the conclusion of the ceremony has been interpreted by many to symbolize the remembrance of sorrow at our moment of greatest joy. It commemorates the destruction of the Temple in Jerusalem, in the year 70 C.E., and reminds us that life consists of both joy and sorrow.

A few additional customs may apply.

- The first is a pre-wedding ceremony called the *badehkin*, during which the bride is veiled by her groom. This can be done privately or in the company of the wedding guests as a pre-wedding ceremony and reminds us of the biblical story of Jacob, who toiled for seven years for his bride Rachel, only to find her older sister Leah when the wedding veil was removed.

- The ketubah is signed before the ceremony. This can be done privately with the rabbi and witnesses or in the view of the guests.

- During the ceremony itself, the bride may circle the groom, recalling a biblical passage which says "A woman shall court a man." (Jeremiah 31:22). She may circle seven times recalling the completeness and the perfection of the creation, or she may circle three times recalling a threefold statement of betrothal from the prophet Hosea 2:21-22. Some brides and grooms now circle one another.

- The groom may be dressed in a kittel, a white robe-like garment, which he will wear over his clothing.

- Following the ceremony, the bride and groom may spend a short time in private, while they eat a light meal. This custom is an important symbolic act, demonstrating the fact that they are married. It goes back to the time when men and women were never alone, unchaperoned, prior to marriage. The eating of a meal alone together thus symbolizes their being alone for the first time as man and wife.

- The families and guests of the bride and groom who are not Jewish are welcome to participate in the wedding ceremony as any Jewish family member or guest would, with the exception of being a signing witness on the ketubah; all signing witnesses must be Jewish adults.

- In the case where a marriage is taking place between a person born to Judaism and a person who has converted to Judaism, this is a marriage between two Jews and is *not* an intermarriage. Both parties are Jewish.

- When one partner to the marriage is Jewish and one is not this is called an intermarriage. Some Reform and some Reconstructionist rabbis will perform this kind of marriage; Conservative and Orthodox rabbis will not. If such a marriage is performed by a rabbi, the non-Jewish partner usually makes some commitments to study Judaism and to include some degree of Jewish observance in the home and in raising the children.

BIRTH

Jewish children are given Hebrew names at birth, in addition to their English names. In the Jewish Askenazik tradition, Jewish children are named after relatives or dear ones who are deceased. According to that tradition, our son Joel is named for Arden's father and grandmother; Diana is named for my grandmothers; and Jordan is named for my great aunt and Arden's great uncle. In the Sephardic tradition Jewish children are named after living relatives.

The most prominent ceremony surrounding a birth in our tradition is the circumcision of the male child, performed on the eighth day after birth. The ceremony is called a *brit milah*, which means covenant, harkening back to when Abraham entered into a covenant with God and circumcised himself as a sign of that covenant. The circumcision is performed by a highly trained person called a *mohel* or, if a mohel is unavailable, by a Jewish doctor under the supervision of a rabbi. Today it is common practice to use a local anaesthetic to relieve the infant of pain. It also relieves the mother of some anguish. The actual circumcision is done in the presence of friends and family who have come for the occasion, but it is not necessary to watch if one does not wish to do so. A brit is an occasion for great joy and celebration in the Jewish tradition. It adds yet another link in the chain of our history, one that is bright with hope for the future.

A part of this ceremony is the giving of the baby's Hebrew name and the special prayer for newborns, also given to girls when they are named. This prayer asks that the baby's life will include *Torah* (learning), *chuppah* (marriage), and *ma'asim tovim* (good deeds).

While there is no specific covenant ceremony for girls, many have been created in recent years, and it is becoming more common to have the same kind of celebration that occurs at a brit (minus any surgical or medical procedure, of course). A covenant ceremony for a girl is called just that, or it may be called a *brit bat* (meaning covenant of a daughter) or *simchat bat* (meaning the celebration of a daughter). The baby girl is given her Hebrew name and friends and family join in the event the same as if the child were a boy. If a covenant ceremony is not held, the baby girl is given her name in synagogue. This is traditionally done the first time the Torah is read after her birth, or at an appropriate service determined by her family and rabbi.

If you attend a brit or a baby naming ceremony, it is appropriate, but not necessary, to bring a baby gift. Anything one might give as a gift to any newborn is appropriate. This is considered in lieu of, rather than in addition to, a regular baby gift. If either ceremony should occur on Shabbat, however, it is not appropriate to bring the gift at that time; instead you can either send it or bring it on another occasion.

Most often, the circumcision ceremony takes place in the home, as does the covenant ceremony for girls. Often a celebratory meal or reception takes place following the ceremony. Depending on your relationship to the family, you might ask if you can bring something to add to the celebrations. This is not expected of guests, however.[2]

BAR AND BAT MITZVAH

Several months ago, I was driving with the radio on when the announcer asked, "If you could pick any day of your life to live over again, what day would it be?" Without missing a beat, the answer came to me instantly, "Joel's bar mitzvah." Not my own wedding, or the birth of my children, but my son Joel's bar mitzvah.

Joel is our first-born child; his bar mitzvah represented a major milestone in my life as an adult, a wife, a mother, a daughter and a granddaughter. It was a point toward which Arden and I had been heading from the time we began to discuss how we would create a meaningful Jewish home and family. It was the moment we had looked toward from the day of Joel's birth. And it was a formal, public statement from us to our community, that we were passing on our tradition to our children.

One memory that is especially precious to me is that of my father, whose synagogue experience was not as traditional as ours, practicing for his grandson's bar mitzvah with him, studying the service in advance and refreshing his Hebrew so he would be up to speed. After he died, we found his study notes for the occasion, which he used for our other children as well.

The ceremony of bar or bat mitzvah is the formal rite of passage into adulthood for Jewish boys and girls. A boy actually becomes a bar mitzvah simply by achieving his thirteenth birthday. For girls, the traditional age of religious adulthood is twelve; today, the decision for the age of bat mitzvah is made by individual synagogues and communities.

According to Jewish law, young men and women are

obligated to observe Jewish laws at this time, whether or not they have a formal ceremony. In common practice, however, one is said to become a bar or bat mitzvah when one is called to the Torah for the first time. In liberal synagogues, both men and women are called to the Torah. The ceremony takes place at any service at which the Torah is read. It most frequently occurs, however, on Shabbat morning. In traditional synagogues, there may not be a ceremony for women, or the bat mitzvah ceremony may take some other form.

The ceremony is the culmination of much effort and preparation on the part of the young person. The requirements and preparations differ, depending on the custom of the synagogue, and the movement of which it is a part. In all cases, however, they include these:

1. the ability to read a certain amount of Hebrew,
2. the understanding of and participation in specific prayers, and
3. the ability to say or chant the appropriate blessings when called to the Torah.

In most cases the bar/bat mitzvah will chant the portion of the service known as the *haftarah* as well. This is a passage taken from the writings of the Prophets that follows the Torah portion; it is a different passage each week. The passage chosen for each haftarah is common throughout Judaism, so on any given Sabbath the same passage will be read in all synagogues.

Often, the choice of who will be called to the Torah to say blessings before the reading is given to the family of the bar/bat mitzvah. Usually the bar/bat mitzvah is seated on the *bima* (pulpit) during the service. Religious honors usually are given to Jewish family members and friends. In many synagogues, provision is made to include family members who are not Jewish. The occasion of a bar/bat mitzvah is an occasion of great joy and celebration. It is a special form of blessing for Jewish parents to see their children take on the faith of their fathers and mothers. It is on this occasion that the bar/bat mitzvah wears a *tallit* for the first time, although in some Orthodox synagogues a man does not wear his own tallit until he marries. After becoming a bar/bat mitzvah young men and women may begin the regular putting on of tefillin for morning services. (While the wearing of a tallit and the putting on of tefillin are customs that are reserved for men in the Orthodox Movement, both men and women in the Conservative Movement have the option, and many exercise it. While not common practice in the Reform Movement, it is an option for both men and women.)

If you are invited to attend a bar/bat mitzvah ceremony, it is customary to give a gift. It need not be a religious item or an expensive one. Anything that is an acceptable gift for a 13-year-old would be appropriate. It is preferable *not* to bring the gift to the synagogue on Shabbat, but you can bring it to the home on the days before the ceremony after the invitation has been received, or to the party if it is held after the Sabbath is over. While it is preferable not to do so in respect of Shabbat, it is not uncommon to see a table set up to receive gifts. Whatever you would wear to a business meeting downtown or to church is suitable attire. It might be helpful to check on the actual time to arrive at the synagogue. Often, the time given on the invitation is for the preliminary service.

DEATH AND MOURNING

When a Jewish person dies, there are clear directions as to how things should proceed with regard to the body, the burial, the funeral, and mourning. The concept of honoring the dead is reflected in all Jewish burial customs. Burial takes place as soon as possible, sometimes within twenty-four hours after death, or as soon thereafter as relatives can gather for the service.

Jewish mourning laws recognize the need for mourning; and they also recognize the need for healing. We are required to mourn intensely for seven days after burial. This period is known as *shiva*, which means seven. During this time one stays at home, sits on low chairs, and wears only slippers or stockings instead of shoes. These are traditional signs of mourning. Mourners also may cover all mirrors and not groom themselves (shave or put on make up) to show the feeling of pain and loss.

Upon returning from the cemetery, it is customary to eat. After the funeral, a meal is served, usually prepared by friends and relatives. Food often is brought to the house of mourning by friends and family during the entire week of shiva to relieve the mourners of the chore of cooking.

Services are held in the home of the deceased on the night of the funeral and for as many nights during the first week as the family desires in liberal families, all nights during shiva (except Shabbat) in Orthodox families. Often, morning services are held in the home, as well. In order for the mourners to say the mourner's prayer, a minyan (quorum) must be present. It is a special mitzvah to ensure that a minyan will be present for the mourners in the home during this period.

The thirty days following the funeral is the period of mourning called *sheloshim* (meaning thirty). During this time, the mourners return to their work, but they refrain from excessive enjoyment such as attending parties, the theater, dances, vacations, and the like.

The Kaddish, (the mourner's prayer) may be said for eleven months less one day after the death of a loved one. This prayer is a part of every synagogue service and therefore is said by the mourner whenever she is attending services. In addition, traditional Jews often go to minyan (daily service) every day, morning and night if it is available, in order to say the prayer every day. In the Orthodox and Conservative traditions, only the mourners rise when the Kaddish prayer is said in synagogue. In the Reform tradition, the whole congregation rises. While this is the general custom, it varies from synagogue to synagogue.

After the eleven months are over, traditionally, the only time the mourners are permitted to say the mourner's prayer is at *Yizkor*, a memorial service that occurs four times during the year on specific holidays, and on the *yahrzeit* of the person's death. In this way, our healing and mourning is defined by degree, with the end goal of returning fully to our lives in society.

Jews do not erect tombstones at the time of death or at the funeral service. In America, this is done some time around the end of the mourning period (eleven months). At this time, the family holds a grave-side service called an unveiling, at which prayers are recited, more words are said about the deceased, and the mourners remove a sheet covering the tombstone, thus unveiling it.

I found these mourning practices to be a great comfort, when my parents and my mother-in-law died. There was a charted course for us to follow. At a time when decisions were difficult, we didn't have to decide what to do when. We just did what was expected, and our healing took place during the process.

Following are descriptions of some Jewish beliefs surrounding death, and specific descriptions of burial practices.

- Judaism does not offer a unified or detailed answer to the question, "Is there life after death?" Jewish belief is based on the biblical phrase from Ecclesiastes, "The dust returns to the earth as it was, and the soul returns to God who gave it." The belief is that "the righteous of all nations have a share in the world to come." Jews believe in the immortality of the soul, and that the soul lives on in the world to come.

- For traditional Jews, there is a burial society to perform the special mitzvot surrounding burial. This group is known as the *chevra kadisha*. Members are responsible for sitting with the body from death until burial, the ritual washing and cleansing of the body, the dressing in a white shroud (and prayer shawl and kippah for men and women who used them), after which the body is placed in a wooden casket without metal ornaments. In the Reform tradition, the clothing for burial and the type of casket is a matter of choice.

- Jewish funeral services may be held in a funeral home,

a cemetery chapel, or a synagogue depending on the wishes and customs of the family of the deceased and the traditions of their particular synagogue or community. Sometimes the family opts for a graveside service. Jewish people are most commonly buried in Jewish cemeteries.

- Prior to the service, traditional Jewish mourners participate in the custom of *kri'a,* which is a symbolic tearing of clothing accompanied by a prayer to symbolize the tear in the heart of a loved one. Typically this is usually done by the rabbi with a knife or scissors, usually on a tie for a man, a scarf for a woman, or on a special "mourner's ribbon".

- For the purpose of kri'a and saying Kaddish, a mourner is defined as one who has lost a mother, father, spouse, son, daughter, sister, or brother.

- The casket is kept closed. Out of respect for the deceased, the body is not seen at the funeral, nor is it viewed at the funeral home.

- The funeral service is conducted by the rabbi. Prayers may be chanted by a cantor, as well. A eulogy is given by the rabbi, and passages are read from Psalms, the Bible, or an appropriate literary source. Members of the family or close friends also may speak. If the deceased is a woman, the passage from Proverbs that describes a woman of valor often is read.

- At the conclusion of the service, the mourners, family, and friends proceed to graveside for the burial. The mourners recite the mourner's prayer, and the casket is lowered into the ground. It is considered a mitzvah for the mourners, friends, and relatives to participate in the ritual of burial by shoveling some earth onto the casket.

- Upon leaving the cemetery, it is customary to wash one's hands. In most traditional cemeteries there is a fountain available for this purpose. Sometimes it is the custom for a "washing bowl" with water to be placed outside the door of the house of mourning after the funeral for this purpose, as well.

- Traditional Judaism applies the biblical edict which states that the body must be buried in the earth. This belief and respect for the body of the deceased are reasons why Jews do not believe in cremation.

- Jews are never buried on Shabbat or Jewish holidays.

- Only Jews are permitted to be buried in Jewish cemeteries. Within the Reform tradition, however, exceptions are made for non-Jewish spouses.

- It is not generally the custom to send flowers to a Jewish funeral, although it is sometimes done. Similarly, it is not customary to bring flowers when visiting the cemetery. Some visitors, however, leave a small stone on the tombstone or the edge of the grave to indicate they have been to visit.

- Jews do not perform autopsies, except in very special circumstances when required by state law, or if an autopsy might help answer questions about the future health of the deceased's heirs. An autopsy is considered a desecration of the body of the deceased.

NOTES

[1] For more information see Anita Diamant, *The New Jewish Wedding Book* (New York: Simon and Schuster, 1985).

[2] For more information, see Anita Diamant, *The New Jewish Baby Book* (Woodstock, VT: Jewish Lights Publishing).

CHAPTER 5

The Holiness of Time
Holidays and the Jewish Calendar

W HILE SOME RELIGIONS and cultures hallow ground with holy places and shrines, and others revere sacred objects which they believe to be holy, it is predominantly through the Jewish calendar and time that Judaism establishes holiness. Holiness in time is established weekly through the observance of Shabbat and through all the other holidays throughout the year, including the first day of every new month, which is set aside for recognition and special prayers. These holidays are set aside for celebration or remembrance and have special readings, prayers, foods, and activities that make them unique. Many Jewish holidays have historical relevance, recalling specific events or times in history. Others—such as the three Pilgrimage festivals: Succot, Pesach, and Shavuot, are also associated with the harvest season.

It is the holiness of time set aside by the calendar which gives Jewish life a special rhythm. The Jewish calendar has shorter months, each with a Hebrew name, and is based predominantly on the moon (as opposed to the secular calendar used by our society, which is based on the sun). To ensure that the holidays will fall in the right season, some extra adjustments are made periodically, by adding an extra month approximately every third year. For this reason, the actual dates of the holidays on the secular calendar may vary from year to year by as much as a few weeks.

All Jewish holidays begin at sundown and end at sundown. This comes from the story of Creation in the Bible, wherein the description of a day's creation concludes with the words: "And there was evening and there was morning the . . . day".

Jewish holidays fall into two categories: *major* and *minor*. The major holidays are those which are specifically mentioned in the Torah: Shabbat, Rosh Hashana, Yom Kippur, Pesach, Shavuot, and Succot. The minor holidays are those *not* mentioned in the Torah: Hanukkah, Tu B'Shvat, Purim, and Tisha B'Av. Two additional holidays have been added to our contemporary calendar: Yom Ha'shoah, the day commemorating the Holocaust, and Yom Ha'atsmaut, Israel Independence Day.

It is customary to introduce the beginning of each major holiday with the lighting of candles. Usually two candles are lit, sometimes more, depending on family custom. The candles are sanctified with a special blessing, and once they have been kindled they are not blown out but instead are allowed to burn all the way down. Traditionally, the candles are lit at least eighteen minutes before the officially stated time of sunset, to avoid the possibility of lighting them after the sun has set and the holiday has begun. This is significant because on some holidays it is not permitted to "make fire" as in the lighting of a match. Doing so after the holiday has begun would be inappropriate. At the official time of sunset on the next day, the holiday is over. The exception to this is the Sabbath, Shabbat, which is not considered to be over until three stars have appeared in the sky. This is true on Yom Kippur as well.

The other custom common to all major holidays, except fast days, is the blessing over wine, or Kiddush. This occurs after candles have been blessed, usually at the beginning of the holiday meal.

Jewish holidays in America may be celebrated for one day longer in the Orthodox and Conservative traditions than in the Reform. This is related to the Jews having left ancient Israel and living in the diaspora, where it wasn't always possible to know exactly when the sun had set in Israel, and the holiday had therefore begun. As a result, holidays in the diaspora often were celebrated for two days to make sure they were being celebrated on the correct day. When Reform Judaism was founded, communication and calendars were much more efficient, and the decision was made to celebrate many holidays for only one day; and, in the case of Passover and Succot, for seven rather than eight.

THE HIGH HOLIDAYS

Most of my life, my yearly calendar began with the return to school. This was true throughout my years as a student, later when I was the school teacher, and finally as a parent when my children were attending school. I remember the excitement of each new beginning, the new shoes and clothing, new teachers, friends, and activities.

The combination of the high holidays and the start of school always represented a special kind of beginning for me. It still does. The whole concept of starting fresh with a clean slate—both literally and figuratively—is one I cherish.

Together, Rosh Hashana (the Jewish New Year) and Yom Kippur, (the Day of Atonement) make up the High Holidays. These holidays come in the Fall, and receive serious attention by almost all Jews, whether or not they are observant during the rest of the year. Unlike most Jewish holidays, the primary focus of observance for the high holidays is the synagogue rather than the home. Most Jews attend services in synagogue, and stay home from work, and keep their children home from school in order to attend.

The ten days from the start of Rosh Hashana to the conclusion of Yom Kippur are referred to as the Days of Awe. This is a time for reflection, for reviewing the old year and preparing for the new. According to a popular Jewish metaphor, on Rosh Hashana it is written in the Book of Life for the coming year who shall live and who shall die and just what the year will bring. While such information is claimed to be *written* on Rosh Hashana, it is believed the Book is *sealed* on Yom Kippur, and therein lies the special significance of the Days of Awe. According to liturgy, "penitence, prayer, and good deeds can annul the severity of the decree." It is to that end that Jews devote their energies during this time.

The first service of the high holiday season is Slichot, conducted on the Saturday night before the holidays begin, to prepare us for the intensity and seriousness of the approaching season. The word Slichot means *forgiveness*. We use this time to ask God for forgiveness for all of our transgressions of the past year, in the hope of building up to the beginning of the New Year, after Yom Kippur, with a clean slate.

The essence of the high holiday season is summed up in one word: *teshuva*. Its meaning is *turning* or *returning*, as in turning yourself around, and changing your behavior from what it has been to the best it can be. The great Jewish philosopher Moses Maimonides said that teshuva occurs when individuals recognize they have erred, choose to correct their behavior, and declare their desire, if only to themselves, not to repeat it.

ROSH HASHANA

According to tradition, Rosh Hashana is the birthday of the world, marking the anniversary of Creation as well as the beginning of the Jewish New Year. Its theme is one of *renewal*. A special liturgy is devoted to the holiday, and much of the traditional liturgy is put to special music.

The *shofar* (ram's horn) is the symbol for Rosh Hashana. The Bible calls Rosh Hashana the day of the sounding of the ram's horn. The sounding of the shofar is our call to conscience, and it is this call that begins the process of teshuva.

Challah, apples, and honey for Rosh Hashana celebtrations.

A child blows the shofar for Rosh Hashana.

Rosh Hashana generally is observed for one day by Reform Jews, and for two by Conservative and Orthodox Jews. The traditional greetings are "L'Shana Tova, ("A good year to you") or "L'Shana Tova Tikateyvu" ("May you be inscribed for a good year"). In addition, at this time many Jews send holiday greeting cards. It is appropriate, but certainly not necessary, for non-Jews to send Rosh Hashana greeting cards to Jewish friends. It is customary to serve foods that symbolize the coming of a sweet year. The most common foods for this purpose are apples dipped in honey and round challah, symbolizing the cycle of life, and usually with raisins baked into it.

YOM KIPPUR

Yom Kippur is the holiest, most solemn day of the Jewish year. It is a day for setting aside normal, everyday activities and work to spend the entire day praying in synagogue, a day for fasting from sundown the night before until the setting of the sun the next day. It is a time for repentance, contemplation, and spiritual renewal, for asking forgiveness for all of our transgressions, both as individuals and as a community. It is a day for trying to bring ourselves closer to perfection, to start fresh and try once again to become the best we can be.

The observance of the holiday begins with the lighting of candles and a prefast meal, to be consumed before the sun sets. The fast is a no-food/no-water fast and is observed by those who have passed the age of bar/bat mitzvah (thirteen years). The evening meal is followed by services at synagogue, sometimes referred to as *Kol Nidre*. The name comes from one of the most special prayers in all of Judaism, a prayer which is chanted that evening. The words Kol Nidre mean all vows. The essence of the prayer asks God to release us from all vows (between man and God, but not between man and man) which we have made, but were unable to keep during the previous year.

The day is spent in synagogue, where the rabbi and cantor are dressed in white and the Torah coverings have been changed to white as well. There is a special liturgy for the holiday, and the tunes of the day are somber. The Yizkor service is recited (one of only four times a year when this is done). The congregation stands many different times during the day to recite the confessional (a long prayer with a list of specific transgressions) and asks for forgiveness. The concluding service as sun sets is called Neilah, which means *locking*. This refers to the closing of the gates of heaven and the last chance to pray for atonement. The services close at the end of the day with a final blowing of the *shofar*. The holiday concludes with a meal known as the break fast.

SUKKOT: THE FESTIVAL OF BOOTHS

Just five days after Yom Kippur, Jews observe the holiday of Sukkot commemorating the period the Israelites wandered and lived in the desert for forty years following the Exodus from Egypt. In the Conservative and Orthodox traditions, Sukkot is celebrated for eight days; in the Reform tradition for seven.

A *sukkah* is a temporary dwelling similar to those in which the Israelites lived as they wandered. Sukkot is the plural form, meaning booths or tabernacles. In celebration of the holiday, each synagogue builds a sukkah for congre-

Welcome to the Family!

Marching on Sukkot with Torah, lulav (palm branches) and etrog (citron).

gational celebration, and some people build them at home as well. It is customary to eat meals in the sukkah, invite friends to visit there, spend leisure time there, and say special blessings for being allowed to dwell there. Some people even sleep in them, weather permitting.

Sukkot is also an agricultural holiday, based on the harvest in the land of Israel. It is a time of thanksgiving for the fruits of the harvest. In fact, it is thought that the Pilgrims modeled the first Thanksgiving on the biblical command to celebrate Sukkot: "When you have gathered in the fruits of the land, you shall keep the feast of the Lord" (Leviticus 23:29).

We are told to gather "four species" of vegetation in celebration of the holiday. These are combined in the *lulav* (a palm branch to which the leaves of the myrtle and willow have been attached) and the etrog (a citron resembling a lemon). Special prayers are recited during the holiday, both in the sukkah and in synagogue, while holding the lulav and etrog, and we march around the synagogue with them in order to give special praise to God.

SIMCHAT TORAH: THE REJOICING OF THE TORAH

Like the high holidays, Simchat Torah is a holiday whose focus is in the synagogue rather than the home. It falls on the day after the last day of Sukkot. Its name means *the rejoicing of the Torah*, and the celebration of the holiday is true to its name. It is a holiday of singing, dancing, and

Celebrating Simchat Torah in the synagogue.

joyous celebration. All of the Torahs are removed from the ark and paraded around the synagogue amid the joyful singing of the congregation. Some dance with the Torah, many dance around it. Children of all ages march in the parade with the adults, waving flags they make in religious school and others they are given upon entering the synagogue.

One of the special things we do in our synagogue is unwrap one entire Torah and open it to be seen by everyone. The Torah is carried to the back of the sanctuary where everyone present stands in a very large circle. The Torah is then opened, a bit at a time and each person holds the top of the scroll until the entire Torah is unwrapped.

Simchat Torah has special significance because of the great value and honor that has always been and still is given the Torah by Jews everywhere. It is on this day that the annual cycle of the reading of the Torah is completed. Each week, a portion of the Torah is read in synagogue. On Simchat Torah, the last verses of Deuteronomy at the end of one Torah scroll are read. Then the first verses of Genesis are read, telling us once again the story of Creation. The annual cycle has begun anew.

HANUKKAH: THE FESTIVAL OF LIGHTS

Our Hanukkah menorah is a traditional one. It is made of brass and is the kind often depicted on greeting cards, with eight branches symmetrically spaced, with the *shammas* (the candle that you light the others with) in the center and a little taller than the rest. The best part about this menorah is that it has a music box inside that plays *Rock of Ages*, the traditional Hanukkah song. Every night during the holiday, after the candles have been lit and the blessings said, we turn on the music box and sing a verse of the song. When our children were at home, they sang, poised and ready to go the minute the song ended. As the last note was sung, they would run to their pile of presents

(Above) Hanukkah candles in various styles of menorot.
(Below) A child lighting Hanukkah candles at home.

and grab the gift they had been waiting all day to open.

Hanukkah is a holiday commemorating religious freedom. The word means dedication and refers to the rededication of the Temple in Jerusalem after its desecration by the Syrian Greeks in the year 167 B.C.E. The Jews' refusal to accept the control imposed on them by King Antiochus resulted in a revolt, led by Judah Maccabee and his brothers, which was one of the earliest recorded struggles for religious freedom in human history. The revolt ended with the retaking of the Temple in Jerusalem, an event which concluded with an eight day celebration in which the Temple was rededicated. We celebrate Hanukkah in honor of this event.

The best-known part of the story is recounted in the Talmud (the commentary of the Torah). It is written that when the Temple was rededicated, there was only one small vessel of purified oil that could be used to relight the great Menorah. That oil should have lasted just one day but miraculously, the oil lasted eight days, until more oil could be prepared. And so we celebrate for eight days.

Hanukkah is spelled several different ways in English, all of which are correct, since there is no absolutely correct form of spelling in transliteration. Often it is spelled Chanukkah with the "ch" at the beginning to copy the sound made in Hebrew (that of the "ch" sound in Bach, not the "ch" sound in Charlie). Other examples are Hanukah, and Hannukka.

In the Jewish calendar, Hanukkah is not one of the major holidays. The attention it receives in North American society is a direct result of its proximity to Christmas. The giving of gifts is also an outgrowth of that influence.

The traditional gifts are coins (*Hanukkah gelt*) which some still give today. Often parents give gifts that are useful, things the child may need anyway; small, fun things rather than major gifts. Traditional Hanukkah gifts are similar to what those who celebrate Christmas call stocking stuffers. If one is so inclined, it is appropriate to send Hanukkah greeting cards to Jewish friends. It is not, however, a traditional Jewish custom to do so.

TU B'SHVAT: THE BIRTHDAY OF THE TREES

Tu B'shvat is known as the birthday of the trees, the new year of the trees, or Jewish Arbor Day. It falls in late January or early February, when the rainy season is ending in Israel. It is celebrated in Israel with the planting of trees. While Tu B'shvat is not a commonly celebrated holiday by most Jews in the United States, those who do celebrate it usually do so with tree planting, by contributing money to The Jewish National Fund (an organization which plants forests in Israel), or with the celebration of a Tu B'Shvat seder, a special service created for the holiday. This holiday is being reclaimed by many Jews today as a way to strengthen their legacy of environmental stewardship and respect. On the holiday itself, Jews often strengthen their connection to Israel and the fruits of the trees by eating fruits, and in particular those fruits which are grown only in Israel.

PURIM: A FESTIVAL OF FREEDOM

Every year as I was growing up, a few weeks before Purim, my Mother, Aunt Gert, and Aunt Rae (and in later years Aunt Jen) would gather to spend a whole day making

Welcome to the Family!

A sofer (scribe) writing the Purim story, or *Megillah*, to be read at the synagogue in celebration of the holiday.

hamentashen (the traditional pastry of Purim). When it was baking day, the aroma in the house had no equal; the house was warm from the ovens going all day, and the sweet dough with a hint of orange peel carried a heavenly fragrance. The end result was hundreds of perfectly shaped, perfectly glazed, and perfectly wonderful hamentashen.

The holiday of Purim, which occurs in February or March, is one of the happiest Jewish holidays and one of the most fun to celebrate. Its source is the biblical book of Esther.

The holiday centers around the events which took place in Persia during the reign of King Ahasuerus. During that time, the freedom of the Jews was threatened by an anti-Semitic villain named Haman, who plotted to have them all killed. The Jews were saved by the intervention of the heroine, Esther, with the assistance of her cousin, Mordechai. Scholars disagree about the authenticity of the story, but it remains symbolically important, whether the events took place exactly as described or not. This is a story of the survival of a people, their courage, and their tenacity.

Jews are expected to read the Purim story, commonly called the *Megillah*, on Purim. This is usually done during services in synagogue, where children—and even some adults!—come dressed in festive costume, ready for fun. When the name of Haman (the villain) is read, everyone stamps their feet, boos, and twirls their *groggers* (noisemakers) in order to drown out his wicked name.

Other customs associated with the holiday are the telling of the story through a Purim Play, contributing *tzedakah* to needy people, the giving of gift baskets filled with sweet treats to friends, and the baking of hamentashen, a three-cornered pastry filled with fruit or poppyseed. Below is my great Aunt Rae's wonderful hamentashen recipe. Enjoy!

RAE ROSEN'S HAMENTASHEN RECIPE

This is the original recipe as given. When there are additional notes in brackets, they are my own comments by virtue of having made them on my own for 41 years.

<u>Prune filling</u>
2 lbs. prunes
2 lb. raisins
1 12-16 oz. pack dates
   [I use the already cut up sugared pieces]
2 pack nuts optional [I do not use nuts]

Baking hamentashen at the synagogue.

> Jam or jelly to taste
> Juice of 1 lemon
> Honey to taste
> 2 oranges, including rind

Put prunes, raisins, dates, and oranges through a food grinder. Mix all together, except honey and jam, by hand. [I literally use my hand] Add the jam and honey last and add as much as is needed to make it sweet, but still retain a bit of the tartness to the taste. Filling can be tasted as you go along with the mixing to decide how much you need.

<u>Dough</u>

12 eggs

[The original recipe was written when the available eggs were much smaller than today's. I usually use 10 instead of 12. One year I used 2 whole eggs and less yolks and it worked fine.]

12 cups peanut oil, or any other oil of your choice

2 cups sugar

2 t. salt

1 t. vanilla

3 cups flour

<u>Method</u>

Beat egg yolks, sugar, and salt until pale lemon in color. Add oil a little at a time while continuing to beat. Then add 2 cups of flour a little at a time, reserving remaining flour for flouring the board on which you roll the dough. [I add more as needed as the dough may be quite sticky. I also sometimes let it chill in the refrigerator before rolling it out.]

Roll out dough till about 1/8 inch thick. Cut into circles. [I use an old wine glass for a cookie cutter to give you an idea of the size.]

Place a teaspoon full of filling on each circle, and then turn up the sides of the circle in thirds so you now have an uncooked pastry that is triangle in shape.

Place on greased cookie sheet. [Original recipe calls for brushing the top of each pastry with egg white. I do not do this.]

Bake for approximately 15 minutes in a 350 degree oven, until slightly browned at the edges.

Pesach (Passover): Remembering the Exodus

I begin thinking about Passover in late January or mid February, about two to three months before it actually occurs. It usually starts something like this: My husband and I are sitting at the dinner table, or driving in the car, and for no particular reason, one of us asks the other,

"Do you think the children are going to come for Passover this year?"

"I don't know. Let's call and make sure they know we want them!"

Or, I come home from the Passover lecture at the Introduction to Judaism class and say to Arden, "You know, we talked about Passover tonight. There are three or four people from the class I want to invite this year."

Before long, I start making lists. I write down the names of those we want to join us. I make lists of the things that need to be done: Call to order tables and chairs, polish all the silver, set aside time on the calendar for cleaning out the cupboards and cooking, start making menus.

If one is traditionally observant of the holiday, preparing the house is a major event. In addition to preparations for the *seder* (the ritual observed at the meal itself), the home must be ritually and thoroughly cleaned, particularly in any places where food has been kept, and rid of all *chametz* (leavened food) of any kind. Preparing the home means changing to a different set of dishes, pots, pans, and of course, we prepare special foods.

Many families rid the household of all chametz. I put mine in the garage or in cupboards that have tape across them. One little piece of chametz is saved and wrapped in a paper napkin to be used later for ceremonial purposes.

On the day of the seder, in the morning before Arden leaves for work, he takes out a feather (which we save from year to year for the purpose) and ceremoniously sweeps a corner of a drawer and a corner of a cupboard to check for bread crumbs. Then he puts the napkin with the chametz in an old metal dish. We go outside on the deck, and there, he pours a drop of lighter fluid in the dish and lights it with a match. As the chametz burns, he recites a prayer that ensures that, even if we do not know it is there, our home is now rid of chametz, both literally and figuratively. We are ready.

Passover commemorates the Exodus of the Jews from Egyptian bondage. This story is central to Jewish worship. Its references are frequent in the liturgy. The story began with Hebrew slavery in Egypt and the cruel treatment they received. Moses, himself a Jew hidden at birth and raised in the house of the Pharaoh, saw the plight of his people and entreated Pharaoh to "Let my people go." When Pharaoh refused, God interceded and brought ten plagues upon the Egyptians. During the seder, we remember all ten plagues: blood, frogs, lice, wild animals, cattle disease, boils, hail, locusts, three days of darkness, death of the first born. As each is named, we either spill a drop of wine onto a dish or dip our finger into a glass of wine to recall that plague.

Overwhelmed by the plagues, Pharaoh finally granted the Jews permission to leave, and they fled Egypt. After their departure, Pharaoh had a change of heart and sent his armies to bring them back. Aware of their peril should they be recaptured, the Jews moved as fast as they could, literally running for their lives. As they approached the Red Sea, a miracle occurred. The sea parted to allow them to cross on dry land. When the Egyptian armies followed in close pursuit, the sea closed and engulfed them, allowing the Jews to gain their freedom.

The story of the Exodus has had a profound effect on Judaism. In fact, during the seder we are told to think of ourselves as having been there, to imagine that we were the slaves who left Egypt. We are told to view the liberation as

Families reenact the Exodus from Egypt in celebration of Passover.

if we were the ones who were liberated, to feel as if we had experienced both slavery and freedom. *"Once we were slaves, now we are free"* is the central message of the holiday.

The observance of the holiday centers around two events: the ritual of the seder, which recreates the story of the Exodus, and the prohibition of eating certain foods during the days of the holiday. The food restrictions symbolize the difficult times of the Jewish slaves prior to and during the Exodus. With these prohibitions, and with specific bitter foods eaten during the seder, we literally taste the bitterness of slavery.

While this description represents the more traditional viewpoint, most Jewish people observe the Passover holiday in a somewhat less strict fashion. However it is celebrated; according to the Council of Jewish Federation's 1990 Jewish Population Survey, Passover is the holiday most celebrated by American Jews. Many have their own seder, attend one at the home of family or friends, or attend a community seder at a synagogue or Jewish community center. Most Jews maintain some food restrictions during the holiday, usually refraining from eating breads and pastries, even if they do not follow the food restrictions to the letter. The foods prohibited during Passover are these:

1. any breads, cakes, biscuits or crackers made with leavening;
2. any leavening agent, such as yeast or baking soda;[1]
3. cereals and beverages derived from grain;
4. any product made with the following items and *not* marked "Kosher for Passover": wheat, barley, oats, rice,

or corn, (including corn oil and margarine); and

5. Dried peas and dried beans.

Many Jewish people simply observe the prohibition against eating bread or rolls. Sephardic Jews eat both legumes and rice on Passover; Ashkenazic Jews do not.

The seder is a family ritual that takes place around the dinner table on the first two nights of Passover for Con-

A seder plate used during the Passover meal.

servative and Orthodox Jews, or on the first with the option for the second for Reform Jews.

During the seder, we read from the *haggadah* which is our guidebook for the ritual. It tells the story of the Exodus and has illustrations as well as the songs and prayers of the holiday. It also tells us which symbolic foods to eat and when during the ritual to eat them. *Haggadot* (plural) commonly used in this country are written in English with some parts in Hebrew, often with transliteration (Hebrew words written with English letters).

Today there are haggadot numbering in the thousands, of every size, kind, and description, written with every type of focus imaginable. A few that we have in our home, in addition to the one we use are: a freedom haggadah, a haggadah for children, an Israel haggadah, an historical haggadah. There are haggadot designed for feminists, gays and lesbians, and variations from the most Jewishly liberal extreme to the most Orthodox. Throughout our history the haggadah has been used as an opportunity for extraordinary creativity with story telling, poetry, art work and illustration.

One of the highlights of the service is the asking of the four questions, traditionally asked by the youngest person at the table. If that person can only say them in English, usually another person will ask them in Hebrew, as well.

The main question is this:

"Why is this night different from all other nights?"

Then follow the four questions:

1. On all other nights we eat leavened or unleavened bread. *Why on this night do we eat only unleavened bread?*

2. On all other nights we eat all kinds of herbs. *Why on this night do we eat only bitter herbs?*

3. On all other nights we are not required to dip at our meal. *Why on this night do we dip twice?* (Dipping refers to putting celery or parsley into salted water. It is literally dipped.)

4. On all other nights we eat either sitting or reclining. *Why on this night do we recline?*

After the four questions have been asked, the haggadah answers them.

One of the favorite rituals of the seder is the children's search for the afikomen, which is a piece of matzah hidden away at the beginning of the meal and saved for dessert. The seder cannot continue until it is found, and the children search for it and receive prizes for their efforts. It becomes a major event for the children, who remember from one year to the next who found it before, and how many times they did or didn't find it.

Another special ritual involves the cup of Elijah. A special cup filled with wine is set aside and placed in a prominent place on the table in anticipation that the biblical prophet Elijah, who is believed to be the harbinger of the Messiah, will come to the seder. At a certain point during the service, we are asked to open the door for Elijah. The legend is that Elijah will come to every seder and drink the wine from his special cup. Each family perpetuates the legend in their own particular way. At our seder, our son Jordan takes all the children outside, walks them down the driveway as far as the mailbox, where all together they call out, very loudly I might add, "Elijah. Elijah." While they are gone, someone pours some wine out of the cup. Imagine the children's amazement on their return to find that the amount of wine in the cup has diminished.

If you are invited to attend a seder, you should be able to follow the haggadah. If you do not understand something, you should feel free to ask questions. You may be asked to participate by reading something. It is not likely you will be asked to do anything that you cannot handle. If much of the ritual is conducted in Hebrew, feel free to ask for the meaning of the Hebrew used. Part of the purpose of the seder is to ask questions about things you do not understand.

If you wish to bring a gift to your host or hostess, it is a good idea to stay away from food items unless you purchase something clearly stamped "Kosher for Passover". (Often such items can be found just prior to and during the holiday in supermarkets in large cities with Jewish populations.) It is usually safer to stick with flowers, a book, pretty paper goods, or something of that nature.

SHAVUOT: RECEIVING THE TEN COMMANDMENTS

Exactly seven weeks to the day after Pesach, we get to eat *blintzes*. That is because it is the custom on the holiday of Shavuot to eat dairy foods, and the general favorite is blintzes.

The word *Shavuot* means weeks, and the holiday occurs exactly seven weeks after the second day of Passover. Its celebration commemorates three things:

1. the giving and receiving of the Torah and the Ten Commandments at Mt. Sinai,
2. the summer harvesting of wheat in Israel, and
3. the ripening of the first summer fruits in Israel.

Clearly the most important part of this holiday is the commemoration of the giving of the Torah, including the Ten Commandments. Although the Bible does not actually associate Shavuot with the giving and receiving of the Ten Commandments on Mt. Sinai, the Talmud rabbinic interpretation and commentary do.

The holiday begins with the traditional festive holiday meal, and continues with holiday services in synagogue. Customs include eating dairy foods (because the Bible likens the holy land to a land of milk and honey), all night sessions studying the Torah, and the reading of the book of Ruth, in which events took place at the time of the harvest.

Contemporary custom in the Reform tradition and in some Conservative and more modern Orthodox synagogues is the ceremony of confirmation. In this ceremony, a religious school class, usually of high school age, participates in a service of celebration after having completed a particular course of study.

Shavuot is observed for two days in the Orthodox and Conservative traditions, one day in the Reform, and is one of the holidays during which Yizkor, the memorial service, is recited.

TISHA B'AV: A JEWISH DAY OF MOURNING

Tisha B'Av falls in late July or early August and is a day set aside to recall several tragic events in Jewish history. Tradition tells us that it was on that day on the Jewish calendar, the ninth of Av, that God decreed the Jews should wander in the desert for forty years. On the same date, the first Temple was destroyed in 586 B.C.E.; the Second Temple was destroyed in the year 70 C.E; King Edward I of England signed the decree expelling the Jews from England in 1290; 150,000 Jews were expelled from Spain by King Ferdinand and Queen Isabella in 1492; and the Warsaw Ghetto finally fell in 1943. Traditionally, it is a day of mourning on which traditional Jews fast. It is not commonly observed by most Jews in the United States.

MODERN HOLIDAYS

Two holidays have been added to the Jewish calendar in the twentieth century: Yom Ha Shoah, honoring the memory of the Holocaust, and Yom Ha'atzmaut, Israel Independence Day. Both holidays commemorate global events that have had an indelible impact on the Jewish world.

These are national holidays in the state of Israel. On Yom Ha'Shoah, at a specific time during the day, wherever you are in Israel you will hear sirens. When they go off, the entire country stops for several minutes. Traffic stops cold, drivers get out of their cars, people stop whatever they are doing and stand silent in the streets in memory of those who were lost to the Holocaust. Yom Ha'aztmaut is celebrated with picnics, parades, and other festivities.

Both holidays are observed throughout the Jewish world outside of Israel, as well. They are celebrated one week apart, usually in late April or early May. In America, they are most commonly marked with community celebrations, often in one synagogue on behalf of the whole community. Both are holidays in which the Jewish community feels a need to come together—the first to mourn, the second to celebrate.

NOTES

[1] According to tradition, the prohibition against leavening commemorates the fact that the Jews left Egypt in such a hurry they were not able to bake bread for the journey. Therefore, we eat matzah to remind us of the flatbread they had to eat on their journey.

CHAPTER 6

Explanations and Definitions

ANSWERS TO COMMON QUESTIONS

WHO IS A JEW?

According to Jewish Law, there are only two ways a person can be considered Jewish: either by being born to a Jewish mother or by conversion after appropriate study and rituals with a rabbi. Recently, the Reform tradition has accepted persons as Jewish by patrilineal descent; if a person is born to a Jewish father and raised in the Jewish tradition experiencing life cycle events, that person can be considered Jewish in this liberal movement.

HOW DOES ONE BECOME JEWISH?

The process of becoming Jewish (commonly used terms are *Jew by choice* or *a convert to Judaism*) varies among each synagogue movement in terms of requirements and length of study. It also may vary among individual rabbis within a specific synagogue movement. The process is similar in all cases, however, in that it requires intensive study with a rabbi. During the course of study, in addition to the Jewish learning which takes place, the person becoming Jewish must think through basic issues of identity. When the rabbi decides the individual is ready, she will be questioned on what she has learned, what her motivation is, and how she will live as a Jew. When possible, this is done by a rabbinical court of three rabbis, called a *beit din;* alternatively, it is done by a board of three people who are knowledgeable, practicing Jews. In the Conservative and Orthodox traditions, requirements for persons becoming Jewish include circumcision for men and immersion in the *mikveh* (ritual bath) for both men and women. The Reform movement has recently adopted new guidelines on conversion, recognizing the traditional practices as well. (These guidelines are voluntary.) If a male is already circumcised prior to his formal entry into Judaism, a symbolic drop of blood is taken from the tip of the penis.

The formal ceremony for becoming Jewish is a simple one, with the person choosing Judaism taking vows attesting to his willingness to take on the Jewish faith. Once that person has gone through this ceremony, *he is a Jew* and thereafter is always considered such. He then no longer adheres to the faith he held prior to this time.

HOW DO JEWS FEEL ABOUT INTERMARRIAGE?

An intermarriage occurs when someone who is Jewish marries someone who is not Jewish. (When a conversion takes place, that person becomes Jewish; if a marriage then occurs it is *not* an intermarriage, it is a marriage between two Jews.)

Rabbis in the Orthodox and Conservative movements do not officiate at weddings of intermarriage. Reform rabbis may do so at their option. Usually they will do so only when there has been some form of Jewish study and a plan for some kind of Jewish future for the home and family.

As intermarriage has become more prevalent, many synagogues and Jewish community centers have begun to offer special programs to the intermarried, recognizing their special needs while still offering them Jewish affiliation and observance as an option.

WHAT DO JEWS BELIEVE ABOUT THE MESSIAH?

Jews believe that the Messiah is yet to come. Traditional Judaism believes that the Messiah will be a descendant of King David, have sovereignty over Israel, will bring the Jews to the land of Israel from all over the world, return the laws of Torah to all Jews, and bring peace to the whole world. The Reform movement does not believe in the coming of the Messiah as an individual. Rather, Reform tradition believes in the coming of a messianic era or utopian age, which will be brought about by the efforts of human beings.

DO JEWS BELIEVE IN JESUS?

No, Jews do *not* believe in Jesus as a divine figure. Jews believe that he was a Jewish man who was a teacher and whose followers created Christianity. They do not believe that he is deified in any way, nor that he is the Messiah.

WHY DON'T JEWS CELEBRATE CHRISTMAS?

Jews do not celebrate Christmas because it is a Christian holiday, commemorating the birth of Jesus whom Jews do not accept either as the son of God or as the Messiah. Therefore, his birthday does not have particular relevance to them.

WHY DO SOME JEWS CELEBRATE CHRISTMAS ANYWAY?

Some Jewish people celebrate parts of the Christmas holiday by virtue of whatever justification they can give, something like, "It really is an American holiday." I share the view of most Jewish people, and certainly the rabbinate, that Christmas is most clearly a *Christian*—not an *American*—holiday, and that it is inappropriate for Jewish people to celebrate it themselves in any way other than wishing their Christian neighbors a happy holiday, or by participating in their celebration with friends outside their home.

"MY CHILD IS MARRIED TO A JEWISH PERSON, AND MY GRANDCHILD IS JEWISH. DOES THAT MEAN I CAN'T GIVE HER CHRISTMAS PRESENTS?"

You need to work this out with your married children, first with regard to them, and then with regard to their children. While you are doing so, you may want to address the topic of Easter celebration or any other relevant religious holidays as well. It is always better to discuss these issues frankly—then everyone can feel better.

SHOULD I INCLUDE MY NEW JEWISH "EXTENDED FAMILY" IN OUR CELEBRATION OF CHRISTMAS?

If you have the kind of relationship in which you share

family events, birthdays, and the like, by all means feel free to invite them to join you for your holiday. I think it is important that you understand that it is *your* holiday, in the same way as if they invited you to share Passover, which is their holiday.

SHOULD I SEND CHRISTMAS CARDS TO MY JEWISH FRIENDS?

I am not offended when I receive a Christmas card, and I always appreciate my Christian friends thinking of me as they are sending out cards to all of their friends. *However*, I especially appreciate those greetings that do *not* refer to Christmas. Remember that Christmas is a Christian holiday, and Jews are not Christians. Therefore, if you wish to remember Jewish friends during the winter holiday season, it is especially thoughtful if you are sensitive about the message on the card you send. Send season's greetings, for instance, or a card that wishes them a happy new year.

WHY DO JEWS FEEL SUCH A STRONG ATTACHMENT TO THE STATE OF ISRAEL?

It is often hard for people who are not Jewish to understand the attachment Jews feel to the land of Israel. The horror of the Holocaust is the climax in a long chain of anti-Semitism and persecution that has followed the Jewish people since earliest times. The need for a strong and secure state of Israel, where any Jew in the world can go to live in safety, is motivated by our history and cannot be separated from it. That is why Jews believe Israel is so crucial. We also believe that *Israel's continued existence must be guaranteed* for Jews anywhere in the world who are persecuted and need a safe haven. Although Jews have a strong national loyalty to the country in which they live, as do their non-Jewish neighbors, Jews also have strong attachments to Israel as a Jewish homeland, and they always will.

JEWISH VIEWS ON CONTEMPORARY TOPICS

While there is seldom one Jewish view on any given subject, (and the views expressed here might be open for some debate within Jewish circles), the rabbis with whom I have spoken generally agree that what appears below is the "Jewish view" on the listed topics.

ABORTION:

Judaism does not approve of abortion as a form of birth control; there must be some mitigating circumstances. Abortion is permitted when the health of the mother, physical or emotional, is in jeopardy.

BIRTH CONTROL:

Liberal views permit virtually all forms of contraception. More traditional views permit those forms of contraception in the woman's control, since the command to "be fruitful and multiply" was given to Adam alone. Some of the most ultra-Orthodox groups do not permit contraception at all.

CAPITAL PUNISHMENT:

There is no "official" Jewish position on capital punishment. However, the laws established by rabbinic commentary regarding capital punishment were designed so that it was virtually impossible to carry out. In practical application today, most Jews are opposed to capital punishment.

DIVORCE:

Although a failed marriage is almost always painful for everyone concerned, Judaism recognizes the necessity of divorce in certain cases. In addition to civil divorce, there is a specific formula for obtaining a Jewish religious divorce. In the Conservative and Orthodox tradition, a Jewish divorce, or *get*, is needed before one can remarry.

ORIGINAL SIN:

Jews do not believe in the concept of original sin. It is believed that all children are born with inherent good, innocent of sin; and sexual intimacy between covenanted partners is seen as a great good. In fact, it is the fulfillment of the first commandment in the Bible: "Be fruitful and multiply."

RIGHT TO DIE:

While the Jewish view is unclear, there is a belief that one has the obligation to sustain life, but not to prolong it; therefore, the view does not insist upon "heroic gestures."

RITUAL OBJECTS

A collection of ritual objects.

CANDLESTICKS:

Shabbat (Sabbath) and holidays begin with the blessing of the candles just before sunset. It is a custom to have special candlesticks for this purpose.

CHALLAH COVER:

Challah is the braided egg bread that is served on Shabbat and holidays. It is customary to keep the challah covered under a cloth, usually decorated for that purpose, until the blessing over the wine has been said,

at which time the bread is uncovered and the blessing over the bread is said.

ETROG AND ETROG HOLDER

An *etrog* is one of the four plant species used in the celebration of Sukkot. It is a citron, resembles a lemon, and has a fragile tip. An *etrog holder* is the decorative case made of wood or metal, with designs or words displayed or carved on it, that holds and displays the etrog during the eight-day holiday of Sukkot. Together with the lulav it is used for special blessings on the holiday.

HANUKKAH MENORAH OR HANUKIYAH

The eight branched menorah used to hold the Hanukkah candles. It has a ninth candle holder, usually in the center and often taller than the others, which holds the special candle (*shamash*) used for lighting the other candles. It is often called a Hanukiyah.

HAVDALAH CANDLE

The candle used for the Havdalah service on Saturday night, which separates the Sabbath from the rest of the week, is braided with intertwined wicks, usually four or six. When it is lit, the wicks burn together so there is one large flame. The lighting of the candle symbolizes not only the end of Shabbat but the beginning of the secular week.

KIDDUSH CUP

A Kiddush cup (or wine cup) is most commonly made of silver. The cup comes in a variety of sizes and shapes, but usually follows the shape of a wine goblet. A Kiddush cup is used when the Kiddush (the blessing over the wine) is said.

KIPPAH (HEBREW) OR *YARMULKE* (YIDDISH)

A kippah or yarmulke is the skull cap worn by men (and sometimes by women) in the synagogue and while praying. This is true of all Orthodox and Conservative males and is an option for Conservative women and Reform men and women. Some also may wear a kippah whenever studying, eating, or in other activities throughout the day. Observant men may wear them all the time.

LULAV

The lulav is the other ritual object used during Sukkot. It includes the other three of the four species used for special celebration on that holiday. The lulav consists of a woven, plaited palm branch to which leaves of myrtle and willow have been attached. Special blessings are said with the lulav and etrog on the holiday.

MEZUZAH, MEZUZOT (PL.)

A mezuzah is a decorative case containing a piece of parchment that is hung on the doorpost of a Jewish home. Its importance is the parchment itself, which is inscribed with verses from the Bible, including the *shema* (a central prayer of Judaism).

SEDER PLATE

On Passover, the focus of the observance is a service at home celebrated around the dinner table, called a seder. The special plate used for this occasion, which has sections for the various objects used in the ritual observance, is called a seder plate.

SHOFAR

The ram's horn, the symbol of the high holidays, is called a shofar. In ancient times, the shofar was used to notify people far away that the holiday had arrived. The timing was passed on from mountain top to mountain top. Today it has significance during the high holiday services as a call to worship.

SPICE BOX

At the conclusion of Shabbat, when three stars appear in the sky, there is a short service that signifies the conclusion of the Sabbath and the beginning of the new week. It is called *Havdalah* which means separation. During the service, three blessings are said: one over wine, one over the spice box filled with sweet- smelling spices to recall the sweetness of the Sabbath day just past, and one over a special candle which is lit at the beginning of the service to symbolize that the week has begun. Special decorative spice boxes are used for this purpose.

TALLIT

A tallit is a prayer shawl worn by Orthodox men, Conser-

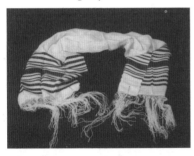

vative men and some women during morning prayers, Shabbat morning services, and services on the day of Yom Kippur. While not a part of the Reform tradition, it is often worn by Reform clergy, and as an option by Reform Jews.

TEFILLIN

Tefillin are two black boxes with leather straps attached which are worn by Orthodox men and Conservative men (and sometimes Conservative women) during the weekday morning prayers. One box is placed on the forehead and the other is placed on the arm, and the straps are wrapped around

the arm seven times. Special quotations from the Torah are written inside the boxes. The wearing of tefillin is biblical in origin. Their purpose is to act as a reminder of man's closeness to God.

TORAH:

The Torah is the scroll of the law, containing the first five books of the Bible.

TZEDAKAH BOX:

A tzedakah box is like a bank in which people put coins to save for righteous giving. The word tzedakah literally means *righteousness*, and is the Jewish term used to refer to charitable giving. It was a custom of old, which some Jews still honor, to put coins in the tzedakah box just before lighting Sabbath candles every week.

YAD:

A yad is the pointer used when someone reads from the scroll of the Torah. It is used so one will not touch the parchment with one's hand, thus protecting the sacred parchment from being soiled.

JEWISH ETHNIC FOODS

They say that memory is influenced by the sense of smell more than by any other. If I close my eyes and go back to my Bubbe's house, I can still smell the foods: fragrance of chicken soup, gefilte fish, roasting chicken with potatoes and onions, and tayglach—a gooey, sticky, honey-covered pastry. The menu may have varied with the holiday, but the savory smells of Bubbe's kitchen were a constant, and so are the Jewish dishes she prepared.

The food descriptions that follow have nothing to do with Jewish dietary laws or with anything religious. Rather, they are special dishes and delicacies that are thought to be distinctly Jewish, all of which (save one) are delicious. These descriptions are based on my own recipes or those of my mother, my mother-in-law, and my grandmothers, or on my experiences of many years of good eating. Like all dishes, they vary from family to family, and because my mothers and grandmothers were Ashkenazic, these specialties are basically Ashkenazic as well.

Although they can be eaten at any time, the recipes fall into three categories:

1. those used traditionally for religious purposes, such as challah (for Shabbat) and matzah (for Passover);
2. those associated with holidays, such as latkes (Hanukkah), hamentashen (Purim), and matzah balls (Pesach); and
3. those foods that are associated with Jews by other folks, and are therefore Jewish *ethnically.*

Bagels are now clearly a part of American society, but they used to be considered a Jewish bread. They are a hard and chewy type of roll shaped like a doughnut.

Blintzes are Jewish crepes. They usually are filled with a white cheese like pot cheese or dry curd cottage cheese, and served with sour cream and berries or jam. They also can be filled with fruit, potatoes, or mushrooms.

Challah is the traditional, braided egg bread that is used for Shabbat and holiday meals.

Chopped herring is a fish delicacy using pickled herring, apples, hard boiled eggs, and bread, all ground up together and served as a spread on bread or crackers.

Chopped liver is Jewish pate made either from chicken or beef liver. In the days before cholesterol consciousness, this delicacy was made even more unhealthy by the addition of chicken fat (*schmaltz*). It may have been terrible for the arteries, but it tasted wonderful!

Cholent is a dish usually made with beef, beans, onions and potatoes. It can be made on Friday afternoon and kept cooking on a very low heat for up to sixteen hours, thus providing a cooked meal midday on Shabbat without breaking the laws of the Sabbath by cooking.

Gefilte fish is not something one loves right away: It is definitely an acquired taste. It is a fish delicacy made with a variety of types of fish which are ground and mixed together. Spices and other ingredients are added, the mix is shaped into patties or balls, and each pattie is boiled in a fish broth. Gefilte fish is commonly served cold as an appetizer, with horse radish.

Hamentashen are special triangular-shaped pastries made in celebration of Purim. The pastries are made of a sweet dough filled with either prune or poppyseed filling.

Kamish bread (or Mandelbroit) is the Jewish version of biscottie. It is usually made with nuts (mandel means almond), and is crisp, not rich, and delicious.

Kasha Varniskes is a combination dish made of kasha (buckwheat groats) and bowtie pasta that is cooked and served as an accompaniment to a meal.

Knishes are another type of pastry that are served to accompany a meal. The dough is something like puff pastry, and the fillings vary from meat or potatoes to rice, spinach or cheese. They usually are served hot.

Kreplach are Jewish ravioli filled with cooked meat or potatoes and onions or a combination thereof. They are boiled, then served in soup, or baked in a casserole and served as a side dish.

Kugel (pronounced "koogle" or "kiggle" depending upon the part of Europe from which the family comes) is a noodle pudding which is served as an accompaniment to a meal. Kugel is made in a casserole, cut into squares, and served hot. While noodle kugel is the most common (and I think the best), potato and spinach kugle are popular also.

Latkes are potato pancakes served on the holiday of Hanukkah. In Israel, however, they celebrate Hanukkah with *sovganiot*— (jelly doughnuts. While mostly you see these served with applesauce or sour cream, my mother's family always served them with sugar.

Lox is a type of smoked or cured salmon, often served with cream cheese on (you guessed it) a bagel.

Matzah, if defined by taste, could hardly be called a delicacy. It is a Jewish specialty food, however. Matzah is similar to a cracker, is baked without leavening, and is used in the celebration of the Passover holiday.

Matzah balls (also called *knaidlach*) are a type of dumpling served in soup, usually chicken soup. They are made from eggs and matzah meal (ground up matzah.)

Tzimmes is a savory dish made with carrots, prunes, and potatoes. It also can be made with meat.

Appendices

I. BLESSINGS

In Judaism, there are blessings for almost everything. They can be said individually or in the company of others. They can be said often during the course of a day (depending on their content); at specific times of the day, week, or calendar, or at a particular moment in time. We always say a special blessing when our children or grandchildren come to visit and sit with us around the dinner table. If blessings are part of an action, such as drinking wine or eating bread, the blessing is said first, and then the act performed.[1]

Almost all blessings begin with the same Hebrew phrase.

Baruch atah Adonai, Elohenu melech ha-olom

"Blessed art Thou, O Lord our God, King of the Universe."

Welcome to the Family!

The translation I have chosen is the traditional one, the one which I was taught as a child and which I still use in my mind and heart when I pray, even though the terms used to refer to God are in the masculine.

Today there are more contemporary translations in use in an attempt to be more gender sensitive, such as:

"Blessed be the Eternal One, Source of Life"

"Holy One of Blessing, Your Presence Fills Creation"

"Blessed are You, Oh God, Source of all Creation"

These are the blessings with which you would be most likely to come in contact. As you read the blessing, use whatever translation works best for you.

BLESSING OVER THE SHABBAT OR HOLIDAY CANDLES

Baruch atah Adonai Elohenu melech ha-olom, asher kid'shanu b'mitzvotav v'tsivanu l'hadlik ner shel Shabbat (*Hanukkah, Yom Tov,* depending on the holiday)

"Blessed art Thou, O Lord our God, King of the Universe, who has sanctified us by your commandments and commanded us to kindle the Sabbath, Hanukkah, or holiday lights."

BLESSING OVER THE WINE

Baruch atah Adonai, Elohenu melech ha-olom, boray p'ree hagafen.

"Blessed art Thou, O Lord our God, King of the Universe, who has created the fruit of the vine."

BLESSING OVER THE BREAD

Baruch atah Adonai, Elohenu melech ha-olom, ha-motzi lechem min ha-aretz.

"Blessed art Thou, O Lord our God, King of the Universe, who brings forth bread from the earth."

BLESSING OF SIGNIFICANT EVENT
(A HOLIDAY, BIRTH, BAR MITZVAH ETC.)

Baruch atah Adonai, Elohenu melech ha-olom, sh-hechiyanu, v'ki-emanu, v'higianu lazman hazeh.

"Blessed art Thou, O Lord our God, King of the Universe, who has kept us in life, sustained us, and brought us to this day."

II. GLOSSARY AND HEBREW PRONUNCIATION GUIDE

Since the Hebrew language is written with Hebrew letters, not English ones, there is no correct English spelling for transliteration. I have tried, however, to use the most common phonetic spellings, and I have used the Sephardi pronunciation, which is the one used in Israel.

There are some sounds which don't translate easily into English, the most common being the sound for "ch". When you see the letters "ch" in written form in a Hebrew word, the sound is pronounced like the "ch" in the name of the composer, "Ba<u>ch</u>": It is *not* pronounced like the "ch" in Charlie.

In some instances I have put additional phonetic explanations following the word listed in the glossary. The following guide will help you in your pronunciation of the rest.

PRONUNCIATION GUIDE

When the following letters appear, they usually sound as they do in the word which is given as an example.
a is pronounced as in father
eh is pronounced as in red
ee is pronounced as in feet
oo is pronounced as in moon
o is pronounced as in boat
i is sometimes pronounced as in feet, sometimes as in big
u is pronounced as in push, unless otherwise stated
ai is pronounced as in buy
ay is pronounced as in say
ei is pronounced as in height
tz is pronounced as in nu<u>ts</u>

GLOSSARY

Afikomen: the "dessert" piece of matzah needed to conclude the Passover seder.

Aliyah: to "go up". It is the term used when someone is called up to the Torah to say the blessings before and after the Torah reading, and the term used for return to Israel, as in one whomoves there.

Anti-semitism: hatred of Jews.

Aron kodesh: the "holy ark," place where the Torah is housed.

Ashkenazim (pl.): those Jews whose ancestors came from eastern Europe; adjective is Ashkenazic.

Aufruf (oofroof): the calling up to the Torah of a groom, or bride and groom for special blessings usually on the Shabbat before the wedding.

Badehkin: a pre-wedding ceremony where the groom veils the bride.

Bar mitzvah: the "son of the commandment," also refers to the ceremony for boys which marks their passage into Jewish adulthood at the age of thirteen.

bat mitzvah: the "daughter of the commandment," also refers to the ceremony for girls which marks their passage into Jewish adulthood at the age of twelve or thirteen.

Bima: the pulpit in the synagogue.

Brachah, (pl. *brachot*): blessing, blessings.

Brit bat: one name given to a covenant ceremony for a baby girls.

Brit milah (bris): the ritual covenant of circumcision.

Cantor: the trained professional who chants prayers in the synagogue.

Chai: life (see l'chaim).

Challah: the traditional braided egg bread which is used on Shabbat and holidays.

Chametz: all bread, leavening, and products which cannot be eaten during Passover.

Chevra Kadisha: an organization whose members prepare a body for ritual burial.

Chuppah: the wedding canopy.

Chutzpa: unmitigated gall, i.e. having the guts to pull off almost anything.

Davening: praying; to daven is to pray.

Diaspora: the places Jews live outside of Israel; a term created from the dispersion of the Jews from their homeland.

Dreidel: a spinning top used for a Hanukkah game.

Etrog: the citron used in the ritual of Sukkot.

Gentile: one who is not Jewish.

Get: a Jewish divorce decree.

Haftorah: portion from the prophetic writings which is chanted on Shabbat following the Torah reading.

Haggadah: the book used for the Passover seder.

Halacha: Jewish law.

Hanukkah: the feast of lights.

Hanukiah: the candle holder used for Hanukkah.

Hamotzi: blessing over the bread.

Hasidim: a sect of Orthodox Jewry who observe the Jewish law in the strictest sense as did their ancestors before them.

Havdalah: a very short service, usually done in the home, at the conclusion of Shabbat when three stars appear in the sky, to say farewell to the Shabbat and welcome the week ahead.

Holocaust: the orchestrated genocide of the Jews by Hitler and the Nazi regime during World War II, resulting in the murder of six million Jews, and many million others.

Kaddish: prayer of praise to God; the same prayer is used for mourners when they say the mourner's Kaddish.

Kashrut: the system of kosher laws, the dietary laws regarding what foods can and cannot be eaten, and how.

Kedusha: holiness.

Ketubah: wedding contract.

Kiddush: the blessing over wine.

Kippah (Hebrew, pl. *kippot*): a skull cap often worn by Jewish men and some women during prayer and at other times. They come in all colors, some very plain and some highly decorated, with stitchery or design.

Kittel: the white coat worn by the groom during a traditional Jewish wedding; worn by some observant Jews on Yom Kippur, and for some other holidays; also used for burial.

Kol Nidre: the special prayer chanted on the evening of Yom Kippur.

Kosher: "fit," refers to those things fit to eat according to Jewish dietary laws.

Kri'a: the custom of tearing or cutting the cloth of some piece of a mourner's clothing or a mourner's ribbon at the time of burial of a loved one.

K'vell: to take great pleasure in.

L'chaim: "to life". Commonly used as a toast when having a drink.

Lulav: (*loolahv*) part of the ritual observance of Sukkot, this is a plaited palm branch to which sprigs of willow and myrtle are attached.

Ma'asim tovim: good deeds.

Magen David: shield of David, the symbol of the six-pointed star often worn by Jews as an adornment, as in a piece of jewelry. Often used as a decorative symbol in synagogues, Jewish art, and ritual objects.

Matzah: unleavened bread, like a cracker, used during the Passover holiday in lieu of bread.

Mehitzah: the separation between men's and women's seating in an Orthodox synagogue.

Mensch: a decent, principled, caring human being.

Menorah: candle holder used in the ancient Temple, recreated as a decorative reminder in many synagogues, also the name most commonly given for the eight branched candle holder that is used on Hanukkah.

Mezuzah: a decorative case, containing a piece of parchment with special prayers, hung on the doorpost of a Jewish home. Its presence signifies that there is holiness within. Often Jews will kiss it as they enter or leave the house by touching first the mezuzah with their fingers and then bringing their fingers to their lips, symbolically taking on the holiness the mezuzah represents.

Mikveh: ritual bath.

Minyan: a quorum of ten adult Jewish persons (men in the Orthodox tradition) required to conduct community worship services. Also used to refer to the service being conducted at the home of a mourner during the shiva (7 day mourning period), and to daily morning and evening services at synagogue.

Mishpacha: family.

Mitzvah (pl. mitzvot): commandment(s). Also translated as good deeds.

Mohel: the person trained to perform ritual circumcision.

Motzi: the prayer said over the bread at the beginning of a meal.

Neilah: (*neelah*) the last service at the end of the day on Yom Kippur.

Ner tamid: the eternal light which hangs over the ark housing the Torah in a synagogue, symbolizing God's eternal presence.

Parashah: weekly portion read each week from the Torah.

Pareve: (also spelled parve) food that is neither meat nor dairy and can be eaten with either, according to Jewish dietary law.

Pesach: holiday commemorating the exodus from Egypt

Pesachdich: referring to foods which are acceptable to be eaten on Pesach.

Pogrom: an organized, planned attack on the Jews of a community, common in eastern Europe, when Jews were beaten, raped, murdered, their property destroyed, usually with government sanction.

Purim: holiday commemorating the deliverance of the Jews from a planned massacre. (See chapter on Purim.)

Rabbi: literally means "teacher," the official term for Jewish clergy.

Rosh Hashana: the high holiday which is the Jewish New Year (see chapter on Rosh Hashana.)

Seder: literally meaning "order," seder is the service done in the home around the dinner table to celebrate Passover, so named because it follows a given order.

Sedra: the weekly portion read each week from the Torah.

Sephardim: (pl.) Those Jews whose ancestors came from

Spain, the southern Mediterranean, or the Arab world; adjective Sephardic.

Shabbat: the Sabbath.

Shalom: peace. Is often used as a greeting for both "hello" and "goodbye."

Shammash: the candle of the Hanukkah menorah, or Hanukiyah, which lights the other candles.

Shavuot: (*Shahvoo-ot*) holiday commemorating the giving of the Ten Commandments.

Shloshim: the 30-day mourning period following the loss of a loved one.

Shema: the central prayer of Judaism declaring faith in one God. The most common translation is, "Hear O Israel, the Lord our God, the Lord is one."

Sheva brachot: the seven blessings chanted at a traditional Jewish wedding.

Shiva: the seven-day mourning period following the loss of a loved one. Traditional Jews sit at home during this time of mourning.

Shofar: ram's horn, the symbol for the holiday of Rosh Hashana.

Shul: Yiddish word for synagogue.

Siddur: prayer book.

Simcha: a joyous occasion.

Simchat bat: a name given to a covenant ceremony for baby girls.

Sofer: the trained scribe who writes the words in the Torah as well as the parchment for Mezuzot (*pl.*) and Tefillin.

Sukkah: a booth decorated with the fruits of the harvest, made for celebrating the holiday of Sukkot.

Sukkot (*Sookot*): the harvest holiday in the fall recalling the times when the ancient Hebrews dwelled in booths.

Tallit: prayer shawl.

Talmud: collection of writings containing a compilation of rabbinic teachings, commentary on the Torah.

Tefillin: two leather boxes, containing prayers, attached to leather straps which are wrapped around the arm and placed on the forehead during the morning prayers by traditional men and some women.

Teshuva: literally, "return," it is the concept of repentance used on the high holy days.

Tikkun olam: the concept of helping in the completion of creation by trying to perfect the world.

Torah: the scroll of the law containing the first five books of the Bible.

Trayf: food that is not kosher, unfit to eat according to Jewish dietary laws.

Tzedakah: literally, "righteousness," and is the Jewish term used for charity.

Unveiling: a ceremony for laying and unveiling a tombstone, usually about 11 months after the death of a loved one.

Yad: Hebrew for "hand." A yad is a pointer, shaped like a hand, used for pointing to the words in the Torah as it is read.

Yahrzeit: anniversary of the death of a loved one on the Hebrew calendar.

Yarmulke: skull cap often worn in prayer by Jewish men and women.

Yeshiva: school for the study of traditional Jewish texts and other Jewish subjects.

Yiddish: language used by the Jews of Eastern Europe, a combination of Hebrew, German, Polish, and the language of whatever country wherein the Jews resided. It is written in Hebrew characters.

Yizkor: memorial service.

Yom Kippur: the Day of Atonement .

Yom Ha'atzmaut: Israel Independence Day.

Yom Ha'Shoah: Holocaust Remembrance Day.

Zionism: the ideology that believes in the need for and continued existence of a Jewish homeland.

III. Suggestions for Further Reading

The books in this reading list were chosen for both their content and readability. I have tried to suggest at least one book to cover each general topic. There are so many wonderful books available, but I intentionally kept this list short so as not to be overwhelming. I hope you will continue your interest in things Jewish by sampling them.

1. *Jewish Literacy,* by Rabbi Joseph Telushkin. (New York: William Morrow, 1948).

If you have only one reference book in your library (in addition to mine of course) or if you want to do additional reading on a variety of topics, this is the book I would recommend. It is an encyclopedic reference book that covers history to contemporary issues and everything in between. The topics are covered in short essay form, and are easy to read. At the conclusion of each essay, the author has included sources for further reading on the subject.

2. *To Life! A Celebration of Jewish Being and Thinking,* by Harold Kushner (Boston: Little, Brown, 1993).

This book describes the Judaism I know and love better than any other. Not only highly informative, it tells the story of Judaism with warmth and feeling in an easily readable, meaningful way. I found myself writing "yes!" in the margins as the author described various aspects of the Jewish experience.

3. *Every Person's Guide to Judaism,* by Stephen J. Einstein and Lydia Kukoff (Northvale, NJ: Jason Aronson, 1991).

This book is just what its title implies: comprehensive. This is an easy book to read from cover to cover or to use for specific topics of interest. Lydia Kukoff is a Jew by choice, and her perspective is especially valuable.

4. *The Jewish Home Advisor: Practical Information and Guidance to All Aspects of Jewish Life* by Alfred J. Kollatch (Middle Village, NY: Jonathan David, 1990).

Also easy to read and understand, its subtitle tells it all.

5. *The New Jewish Wedding,* by Anita Diamant (New York: Simon and Schuster, 1985) and *The New Jewish Baby Book,* by Anita Diamant (Woodstock, VT: Jewish Lights, 1985).

These are highly recommended, informative, and interesting books, describing in an all-inclusive manner the topics of weddings and babies and the customs surrounding them. One of the special features of both books is the creation of new rituals and new twists on old ones to accommodate intermarriage, Jews by choice, and the expanding role of women.

6. The *Jewish Dietary Laws,* by Rabbi Samuel Dresner (New York: Burning Bush Press, 1949).

If you are seeking a comprehensive description of

kashrut, this is the book for you. It will tell you what you need to do to have a kosher home, plus all you will ever need to know about the Jewish dietary laws.

7. *Shabbat,* by Abraham Joshua Heschel (New York: Farrar, Straus and Giroux, 1951).

Clearly the most beautiful book about Shabbat one can read, poetic in style; One can almost feel the peace of Shabbat within its pages. Its approach is philosophical and mystical as well as informative. If you haven't observed Shabbat before, you will want to when you are finished reading it.

8. *All But My Life,* by Gerda Klein (New York: Hill and Wang, 1957).

All But My Life is an autobiographical account of one woman's experience during the Holocaust. While there are many books to be recommended on this subject, I believe this one to be the best. It is beautifully written and, unlike many, tells its story in a way we can relate to and understand. Gerda's story is also portrayed in a documentary that won the 1996 Academy Award. It is shown at the National Holocaust Museum in Washington, D.C.

9. *The Jewish Way in Death and Mourning,* by Maurice Lamm (Middle Village, NY: Jonathan David, 1969).

Written from a traditional perspective, the author covers the topic completely in a readable fashion.

10. *Heritage: The Civilization of the Jews,* by Abba Eban (New York: Summit Books, 1984).

In addition to providing Jewish historical background,

Heritage also tells the story of the Jews' impact on civilization and of world history's impact on the Jewish people. This is also available on video from the television series which was created from the book when it was first published.

11. Wanderings by Chaim Potok. New York: Ballentine Books, 1984.

A good comprehensive coverage of Jewish history, *Wanderings* is the history book we use in the Introduction to Judaism class.

NOTES

[1] The exception to this is the blessing of the candles, which are first lit, then blessed. Because it is necessary to strike fire before the start of Shabbat in order not do be doing "work" on the holiday, if the blessing were said first, the lighting of the match would occur after the beginning of the holiday, when it would be inappropriate to strike a match.

Dear Reader,

I would love to hear from you. I am interested in your reactions to my book, and will appreciate your feedback, ideas, and experiences related to *Welcome to the Family!* I promise I will answer you.

My e-mail address is: Lois@WelcomeToFamily.com

My mailing address is: Lois Shenker
                          PO Box 19390
                          Portland OR 97280

Please check out my web site at:
www.WelcomeToFamily.com
There you will find discussion questions for book clubs, speaking topics, and links of interest.

Thanks so much. I look forward to hearing from you.

                    Lois Shenker